Gifted Children in the Regular Classroom

The Complete Guide for Teachers and Administrators

by Kathryn T. Hegeman, Ed.D.

Special Consultant: Dr. Anne L. Corn
Department of Special Education
University of Texas at Austin

Fourteenth Printing

Royal Fireworks Press
Unionville, New York
Toronto, Ontario

Acknowledgements are due to my colleagues, *Maryann Llewellyn* and *Judith Goffhelf*, for their encouragement, support and help.

Appreciation and a special note of thanks for their review of the section on **The Gifted Child Individual Education Plan (IEP)** go to *Alvin Migdal*, Director, and *Joseph T. Haward*, Administrative Assistant, Special Education, Board of Cooperative Educational Services, First Supervisory District, Suffolk County, New York.

Illustrations by *Mark S. Hegeman* and *Dana Tillinghast.*

Royal Fireworks Press
First Avenue, PO Box 399
Unionville, NY 10988-0399
(914) 726-4444
FAX: (914) 726-3824
email: rfpress@ny.frontiercomm.net

Royal Fireworks Press
78 Biddeford St
Downsview, Ontario
M3H 1K4 Canada
FAX: (416) 433-3010

ISBN: 0-89824-023-9

Printed in the United States of America on acid-free, recycled paper using soy-based inks by the Royal Fireworks Printing Company of Unionville New York.

TABLE OF CONTENTS

Foreword

Teachers have an insatiable appetite for practical, what-to-do-and-how-to-do-it ideas for the classroom. And understandably, too, considering the sheer number of instructional acts they produce on a regular basis. It boggles the mind to contemplate how thick a "script" has to be for "staging" an educational program five hours a day, 180 days a year, for 25 to 35 children, each of whom requires separate improvisations in methods and materials. No wonder that so many promising practices are adopted uncritically by teachers who live in constant worry that their classroom repertoire is never rich and varied enough to suit their children's needs.

The gifted are especially apt to tax a teacher's stock-in-trade because of the huge varieties and amounts of curriculum content they consume and because of the special strategies required to determine who can benefit from enrichment, how to administer it, and what approaches to take in evaluating its quality. As interest in the gifted grows, teachers demand more and more resources to make differentiated education possible. There is already an increasing flow of to-be-used-with-the-gifted materials into classrooms, some of them ingenious, others fatuous though put together in deceptively slick packages. It is hard to care about discriminating between the good and the bad when you need all the help you can get.

Kathryn Hegeman's manual adds not only to the quantity of practical resources for teachers of the gifted, but, far more important, to the quality, too. Mrs. Hegeman is a virtuoso teacher and teacher trainer who has worked successfully with gifted children. Her experience in the classroom has yielded many of the ideas contained in this volume, and teachers should welcome the opportunity to benefit from a creative educator's assistance. For all would agree, an existing invention is preferable to the wastefulness of repeated re-invention. Why plan afresh for every site when it is so much more efficient to benefit from the excellent plans that Kathryn Hegeman has already designed, tested, and recorded?

The manual is not just a collection of tricks for the trade without a conceptual foundation. Besides being an outstanding practitioner, Kathryn Hegeman is a sound student of the nature and needs of the gifted. She knows the theory, the research, and the target population. For that reason, she is capable of investing her practical, day-to-day classroom activities with intellectual insight and integrity. Teachers can rest assured that the manual was prepared by a highly qualified specialist in her field, NOT an idea person who sees a ready market for any material that bears the label, "made for teachers of the gifted."

Abraham J. Tannenbaum
Professor of Education
Teachers College, Columbia University

chapter 1

INTRODUCING THE GUIDE

Enrichment of Gifted Children in the Classroom

This book is a step-by-step guide; it provides a program to meet the needs of gifted children in the regular elementary classroom. It is intended primarily for use by the classroom teacher, but administrators, specialists, and parents will find it helpful.

It provides specific details for meeting the special needs of the gifted individually, in a small group, or with the whole class. Effective plans and processes for program organization, explained.

Reproducible identification checklists, assessment records, forms for individual education plans, and other helpful devices are included.

A partial listing of topics:
- Program overview on the district/school and classroom level
- Parent information and advisement
- Nature and needs of the gifted child—identification
- Specific teaching/learning strategies
- Differentiated instruction
- Tips for the primary teacher
- Tips for the teacher of children in grades 4-6
- Evaluating pupil progress
- Enrichment planning
- Community/mentor talent bank.

This book is based on the premise that a program for gifted children can begin with attention to the gifted children in every regular classroom. Emphasis will be placed on how a teacher can identify special needs and provide the personalized, differentiated learning experiences so vital to gifted children.

Even when schools have made certain limited provisions for the gifted students (i.e., part-time resource room activities), the fact remains that many gifted youngsters spend the major portion of their time in their homerooms. The classroom teacher must assess developmental needs, provide suitable instruction, guidance, and emotional support. Each gifted child must be dealt with as a unique individual who differs from other children in his/her particular aspects of giftedness.

Children also differ in background and experiences; a rich and nurturing classroom environment allows gifts and talents to be identified for cultivation. Children also vary in many aspects of development. Classroom enrichment supports an ongoing identification process by encouraging children to develop their abilities and deal with their disabilities while they gain in maturity and experience.

The process of coordinating and implementing a policy of classroom enrichment offers minimal problems to the school administrator. It requires involvement, support services, and evaluation procedures.

A comprehensive written plan that clearly articulates philosophy, goals, and identification procedures must be developed by the school district. The structure of the self-contained class can meet individual needs, providing skilled teachers are adequately supported with human and material resources. The success of any organizational plan depends finally on the classroom teacher's ability and creative use of time, space, and materials.

Encouraging good teachers to pursue goals of excellence in their professional skills enables them to provide challenge in the classroom and serve as stimulating role models for bright and able youngsters.

This book directly confronts a number of ethical questions. How do we meet the needs of the gifted child without removing leadership potential from the classroom? How can a busy teacher work with all ability levels without compromising certain individual needs? Who is the gifted child? What is the school's responsibility? How can parents help their gifted and talented children? Or better yet, how can parents encourage children to develop their gifts and talents?

This manual provides tested approaches and activities which not only stimulate gifted children but also enhance the learning environment for all children.

The many practical suggestions presented here are not intended as a restrictive model for teaching gifted students. They are, rather, strategies to develop the framework for enrichment that can be adapted to the needs of many gifted children, their teachers, parents, and communities.

This manual can be used effectively in a number of ways. For the individual teacher, it contains ideas and suggestions for learning activities suitable for gifted children. It can serve as a dynamic base for an informal teacher study-group. For school districts, it can be a valuable component of in-service education for teachers of the gifted.

While programs will, of course, differ in design, certain elements are non-negotiable. These essential components of a systematic, district-wide approach are reviewed in detail.

Objectives

To provide the classroom teacher with the ability to:
— identify gifted children in their classrooms by using checklists and information-gathering techniques.
— evaluate their own potential for working with gifted children and be able to augment their abilities.
— utilize methods in differentiating instruction at the primary and intermediate levels.
— facilitate cooperation with parents and other teachers.
— become effective team members in developing the gifted child's education plan.
— be able to monitor the gifted child's needs on an ongoing basis.
— locate and select appropriate materials for classroom use.
— identify potential giftedness in youngsters who might otherwise go unnoticed.
— utilize community resources to extend and supplement classroom activities.
— utilize evaluation and classroom management techniques.

chapter 2

AN OVERVIEW OF SYSTEMATIC SCHOOL DISTRICT PROGRAMMING

School District Program Planning

A major goal of this book is to provide a model for a district-wide comprehensive program for gifted children in the regular classroom. Too often guidelines for a policy of classroom enrichment are left vague and undefined. Coordinated efforts to maximize support services and extend enrichment opportunities require that administrators deal with specific concerns in detail. The necessary information, helpful forms, and management procedures are in this section.

When everyone within a school district realizes how vital her/his commitment is in developing a network of support, teacher competence in dealing with the gifted child is an attainable goal. This section also provides an overview of some important issues for a school district drawing up a clear and concise educational policy for the gifted.

A suitable program must:
— formulate a clearly defined statement of the school's philosophy, goals, and objectives for the gifted student.
— establish adequate identification procedures for all gifted students, including the disabled.
— provide in-service training, information, resources, and materials for the staff.
— develop differentiated curricula to meet the individual needs of the gifted student.
— provide for parent information, advisement, and conferences.
— establish adequate ongoing evaluation procedures.
— extend the horizons of the gifted by utilizing community resources.

Provisions for the gifted must become an integral part of the regular school program, weaving a web of enrichment that both encompasses and extends the basics.

Formulate a Clearly Defined Statement of the School's Philosophy, Goals, and Objectives for the Gifted.

Local school districts have the primary responsibility for meeting the needs of their gifted pupils. They should provide "equality of opportunity" so that gifted youngsters can achieve their potential.

A broad-based committee should be formed to review existing procedures for the education of gifted children within the school district. After assessing current practices, the committee should draft a plan to be approved by the local board, that initiates, modifies, or extends a sound educational program for gifted students.

The plan should show a sensitivity to and awareness of the nature and needs of gifted children. It should also include a comprehensive program of differentiated learning experiences.

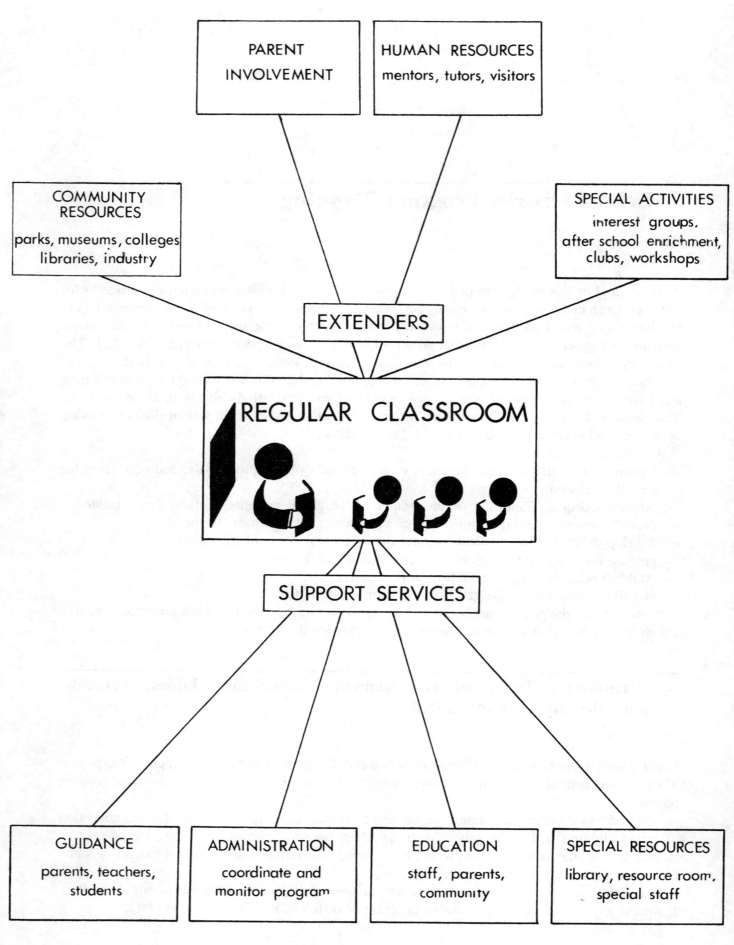

PARENT
INVOLVEMENT

HUMAN RESOURCES
mentors, tutors, visitors

COMMUNITY
RESOURCES

parks, museums, colleges
libraries, industry

SPECIAL ACTIVITIES
interest groups,
after school enrichment,
clubs, workshops

EXTENDERS

REGULAR CLASSROOM

SUPPORT SERVICES

GUIDANCE
parents, teachers,
students

ADMINISTRATION
coordinate and
monitor program

EDUCATION
staff, parents,
community

SPECIAL RESOURCES
library, resource room,
special staff

Communities vary greatly and the differences will be reflected in the responses of the schools to the needs of gifted students.

Even though programs may vary in emphasis and structure, certain key elements must form the core of any plan for gifted children. Essentially, these humanistic goals seek to help gifted children develop into intellectually capable, productive, and sensitive human beings.

The plan must:
— focus on a child-oriented approach that considers the individual as the basis for organization.
— provide opportunities that develop leadership qualities.
— emphasize the learning process itself in order to foster the ability to adapt creatively to change.
— encourage personal growth and intellectual challenge.
— help children develop a sense of moral responsibility and positive values.
— offer guidance and support to help gifted children achieve emotional well-being and a positive self-image.
— establish a systematic method to monitor pupil progress regularly from K through 12.
— coordinate objectives, scope, and sequence in all curricular areas from K through 12.
— utilize community resources to expand the horizons of the gifted children.

Establish Adequate Identification Procedures for All Gifted Students, Including the Disabled

Who is the gifted child? From an operational viewpoint, a child with great innate ability, exceptional talents, and/or superior potential for achievement requires educational services beyond the scope of the regular school program.

It is essential that teachers receive information on the nature, needs, and traits of the gifted child, since the identification process is essentially bound up with the teaching/learning environment. Flexible and open screening policies should be maintained. Children must be given opportunities to produce and demonstrate their giftedness and potential in any specific area. In working to increase opportunities for the gifted child, teachers will actually be improving the educational climate for all children.

The classroom teacher should be aware of the many clues that gifted children themselves provide to their unique abilities.

Schools need not necessarily embark on lengthy and expensive testing procedures. They must, however, assess current diagnostic/testing practices and support the staff with an adequate in-service program on education of the gifted.

There should be a commitment to identify all gifted students with the primary objective of developing their capacities to the fullest extent possible. Early identification of gifted students should be stressed. This outlook encourages the development of an individualized education plan (IEP) for each gifted child.

This approach assures that children will be exposed to differentiated curricula and strategies suited to an individual's growth rate, needs, and abilities. An analysis of student achievement, interests, and innate ability are all involved.

Specific and multiple criteria are to be used, employing both standardized and informal tests that may include:

readiness tests
I.Q. tests
rating scales for gifted students
rating scales for identifying creative potential

achievement tests

teacher evaluation

student interest inventory

peer nomination

sociograms

information from parents and other sources

work samples.

Those children in need of a special program can be determined on an individual basis by the administration and/or committee in consultation with classroom teachers and parents. Great care should be used in considering disabled, culturally different, and underachieving students; their giftedness often goes unnoticed.

The identification process should be ongoing because growth and development brings out new facets in children. Also, many families move frequently, and a flexible approach is necessary to assess children moving into the school district. This requires that procedures be set up to assure prompt attention to diagnosing needs and prescribing a suitable individual education plan (IEP).

When screening for potential giftedness in new arrivals, consideration must be given to the following:

— prior performance and school records

— a team approach to evaluating and testing incoming students

— input from the classroom teacher including informal tests, measures, and observations (e.g., checklists)

— input from parents.

Screening and identification should be accomplished as soon after entry as is reasonable.

Provide In-Service Training, Information, and Resources for Staff

The key to any successful program for the gifted lies with the classroom teacher. For the program to work, it must include the classroom teacher in the formulation, implementation, and evaluation.

The strategies outlined here depend upon the overall developmental pattern of the gifted child and to assess how the child functions within the learning environment. The teacher is in a unique position to diagnose, prescribe, and monitor the child's progress. How does the child react to program plans? The plan may need revision as the child reacts to it. The needs of each child are accommodated by adjusting the curriculum through skills taught, content used, and modality (by which the child most readily learns) employed.

The administration and board must respond to the needs of the educator in the classroom. They should assist the teaching staff with human and financial resources: in-service training, information, materials, and support services.

Priorities for in-service training should include but not necessarily be limited to the following:

— assessment of current practices and teacher needs

— awareness sessions on the nature, needs, and traits of the gifted

— specifics of identification procedures

— information on specific curricula design and teaching/learning strategies for the gifted

— evaluation procedures

— resources, materials, and support services for staff and special student needs

These areas of concern may be developed through a variety of approaches:
— attending in-service workshops
— working with consulting services
— establishing a well-stocked and staffed teacher resource center for the dissemination of materials, books, and periodicals
— attending courses and conferences on the gifted at local colleges and universities
— visiting other programs

The following questionnaire is designed to assess current staff needs.

Develop Differentiated Curricula To Meet the Individual Needs of the Gifted Child.

A school district's goals for the education of gifted children should be similar to those for all children. After all, gifted children pass through the same stages of development and need affection, security, and growth toward independence.

The curricula of a program for gifted children are based upon the regular school program. Adaptations in curricula plans are concerned basically with meeting individual needs.

Clearly defined goals for differentiating curricula provide a framework for parents, teachers, and children and a method for measuring progress. What are some worthwhile goals for a policy of enrichment in the regular classroom? Strategies and methods should be developed in order to:
— develop an individual education plan (IEP)
— accommodate individual needs through curriculum adjustment
— allow a child to move ahead according to his/her developmental rate
— offer guidance and support to children at every stage of growth
— broaden and deepen the learning experience
— encourage creativity and problem-solving abilities
— assure mastery and expansion of basic skills
— promote higher-level thinking skills
— extend horizons beyond the classroom
— provide opportunities for leadership qualities to develop

The school community should applaud the development of learning alternatives which are designed to encourage growth at varying levels of abilities, interests, and needs.

As staff members think about their concerns for these bright and able students, they will find many more questions will be raised. Teachers will develop focus, purpose, and a new sense of direction as advocates for gifted children.

This will no doubt enhance the educational environment for all students as activities develop and suggest new directions for learning. A qualified, enthusiastic teacher is the key to providing a receptive learning environment for the gifted child.

QUESTIONNAIRE: PROGRAM FOR THE GIFTED CHILD

1. How would you describe a "gifted child?"

2. How have you effectively handled your bright students within the classroom?

3. How could parents, the school board, and interested community members assist in development programs for the gifted?

4. How would you use auxiliary personnel, if available, to work with gifted children?

5. In what area do you feel you could most use help in working with gifted children?

6. If extra resources were available, to which three items would you give priority in meeting the needs of gifted children?

7. What additional training do you feel would prove beneficial for teachers to enable them to better meet the needs of gifted children?

8. What future plans do you have to accommodate the needs of the gifted children within your classroom?

Books That Inform

Delp, Jeanne L., Martinson, Ruth A. *The Gifted and Talented: A Handbook for Parents*. Ventura, California: National/State Leadership Training Institute on the Gifted & Talented, 1975.

Ehrlich, Virginia Z.: *The Gifted Child: A Handbood for Parents and Teachers*. New York: Trillium Press, 1985.

Kaufmann, Felice: *Your Gifted Child and You*. Reston, Virginia: Council for Exceptional Children, 1976.

Simon, Sidney G. & Olds, Sally W.: *Helping Your Child Learn Right from Wrong: A guide to Values Calrification*. New York, McGraw-Hill Paperbacks, 1977.

Smith, Jamie C.: *Beginning Early: Adult Responsibilities To Gifted Young Children*. New York: Trillium Press, 1986.

Valentine, Deborah: *Educational Play: Language Arts*. New York: Trillium Press, 1986.

Webb, J. T. et. al.: *Guiding the Gifted Child: A Practical Source for Parents and Teachers*. Columbus, Ohio: Ohio Publishing Co., 1982.

ORGANIZATIONS THAT CARE

*The Association for the Gifted (Journal for the Education of the Gifted) c/o The Council for Exceptional Children 1920 Association Drive Reston, VA 22091.

National Association for Gifted Children (The Gifted Child Quarterly) 4175 Lovewll Rd, Circle Pines MN 55014.

Action for Children's Television, Inc. (ACT 46 Austin Street, Newtonville, MA 02160.

Trillium Press, Parent Services Division, PO Box 209, Monroe NY 10950 (914) 783-2999.

*(write for information about local chapters/affiliates)

Pamphlet For Parents

THE GIFTED CHILD NEEDS

PARENTS AND TEACHERS WHO

Work together

Help enrich

Offer support

Who Is the Gifted Child?

The gifted child is found in all segments of society. These children show exceptional ability or potential in many areas and require a differentiated educational program.

The gifted child often demonstrates outstanding intellectual ability and specific academic aptitude.

Many children demonstrate creative potential while others show superior talent or ability in many specialized areas such as art and music.

Gifted children provide many clues to their own high ability. Parents and teachers should be aware of these clues.

Gifted children may posses some of the following behavioral or personality traits:
- early language proficiency
- early development of reading ability
- curiosity
- an observant nature
- longer than usual attention span
- the ability to retains and apply information
- early discovery of cause and effect relationships
- creativity
- an interest in many things
- special talent

Remember the gifted child needs freedom to play, explore and daydream as all children do.

Care must be taken neither to overestimate nor underestimate the ability or potential of any child, including the disabled or culturally different.

What Is the Responsibility of the School Toward the Gifted Child?

The school should provide equality of opportunity for the gifted child.

A comprehensive plan of differentiated education for gifted children is necessary if they are to reach their potential.

To ensure this, a school must consider many factors such as:
- Formulating a clearly defined statement of the school's philosophy, goals and objectives for the gifted.
- Establishing adequate identification procedures.
- Developing strategies and differentiated curricula to meet the individual needs of the gifted.
- Providing in-service training, information, resources and materials.
- Cooperating with educators, parents, and associations to advance the cause of quality education for the gifted.
- Establishing evaluation procedures.
- Provisions for parent information, advisement and conferences.
- Expanding horizons beyond the classroom.

The school must help gifted children become worthwhile individuals, realize their potential, and contribute to society.

How Can Parents Help Their Gifted Child?

Children grow and learn through experience.

The home life of a child determines the extent and nature of a child's early learning opportunities and indeed shapes the child's interests and goals.

An enriched home environment is the key factor that sparks creativity and encourages intellectual development.

Creating a home environment that is supportive and nurtures a child's abilities without pressure is worthy of the parents' efforts.

An environment that fosters learning provides:
- opportunities to develop positive values and attitudes.
- motivation and encouragement.
- opportunities to interact with thoughtful answers to the child's questions.
- ways to build on the child's interests.
- opportunities to discuss and analyze current topics.
- guidance and support.
- opportunities for a variety of social experiences.

Parents are teachers too! Share a special interest of yours with your child, a truly joyous learning experience for both of you.

Take time to plan special trips to enhance and enrich your family life. Utilize community resources and cultural programs.

Maintain an interest in your child's school work and progress. Encourage your child to take independent action and adopt responsible behavior.

Become involved in groups that promote the education of gifted and talented children.

Provide for Parent Information, Advisement, and Conferences

Parents are concerned with the educational needs of their gifted child. They want to know what the school's responsibility is and how they can help.

The school policy should encourage maintaining open lines of communication between parents and teachers. Every effort should be made to give parents information about their child's strengths, weaknesses, and potential for achievement. Input from parents detailing their child's interests and behavior is exceptionally valuable. Parents should be considered an important part of the planning process for their child's educational program. When informed about the school program parents can provide enrichment and extend the child's learning experiences.

Establishing a working rapport with parents can be achieved through many avenues such as conferences, seminars, newsletters, progress reports, school visitations, and group discussions.

Support services for parents are important if they are to deal with parental concerns, such as underachievement, avoidance of pressure to perform, shyness, isolation from peers, and lack of community resources.

The school may wish to make information available concerning the parents' role through an information brochure such as the one in this chapter. You can reproduce it and send it home as a pamphlet.

Parental activity varies from community to community and even within a school district itself. There are many reasons that parents do not become involved: language barriers, socio-economic conditions, time constraints (due to large families, single-parent homes, or both parents working). The parents themselves may have unpleasant memories of their own school days and feel ill at ease in their children's school.

Administrators and teachers cannot simply throw up their hands and abandon efforts to establish a working relationship with parents. Extra communication efforts will not only aid the individual child, but also go a long way toward increasing support for the school and its programs. For parents who are unable to attend general meetings or workshops, an outline or notes on the meeting may be sent home in the form of a newsletter. Parental interaction may be encouraged through:

flexible schedules
newsletters
home visits
report cards
work folders and comments
progress reports
an open house
workshops on parenting
discussion groups
conferences
visitation days
a showcase of children's activities (projects, writing, art, music, science, drama, physical education)

The important factor is to keep the lines of communication open and try to consider any suggestions parents make on program plans and policy.

Establish Adequate Evaluation Procedures

Evaluation is a vital element when any special school program is being developed. Procedures should maintain continuous, ongoing evaluation among those most concerned: the administrator, the parents, and the teachers.

Evaluation procedures should provide the following information:

PARENTS — A comprehensive analysis of their child's progress which notes strengths, weaknesses, and potential for achievement. The child's affective needs, interests and motivation should be discussed.

THE TEACHER — An account of how the child is performing and reacting to his/her individual education plan. This ongoing assessment provides a basis for future planning for both cognitive and affective needs. Data on a child's behavior serves as a reference point in discussing the child's progress with others.

GIFTED CHILD — Self assessments of: how he or she is doing and feels about him or her self; what his or her interests and strengths are; and where extra help and practice are needed.

ADMINISTRATOR — Assessments of how the teacher is monitoring and evaluating individual pupil progress; how resources, support personnel, and materials can be organized to meet specific needs; how well the classroom climate, curricular modifications and overall program modifications relate to the program's basic objectives.

A systematic and organized method of evaluating student progress should be developed along the following lines:

- Classroom teachers should assess the overall developmental pattern of each gifted child and judge how that child functions within his or her learning environment.
- Teachers should outline an individualized education plan for each gifted child in conjunction with his or her parents and the IEP Committee.
- The Administrator and/or the IEP Committee should meet with teachers at regular intervals in order to discuss the gifted child's program and progress throughout the school year.
- Continuing support, advisement and information can be offered to parents as they are informed of their gifted child's progress.
- An individualized, cumulative record of progress and development may be kept on each gifted pupil.
- Teachers may plan enrichment opportunities to extend child's horizons (library, resource room, mentor program, special interest clubs, mini-courses, etc.).
- Resource staff and teachers should cooperate in planning student activities and monitoring the child's progress.
- The child's progress and development folder, which includes work samples, skills, checklists, teacher evaluations, records of achievement, and other pertinent information should also be reviewed periodically.
- Students should be encouraged to evaluate their own academic progress and participate in activities planning. Self-evaluation of personal growth should be included.

A brief self-evaluation form for classroom teachers follows.

TEACHER SELF-QUIZ ON CLASSROOM PROVISIONS FOR THE GIFTED CHILD

Your brief but thoughtful responses to the following questions will help you assess current provisions for the gifted child in your classroom.

1. Can I define a gifted child and readily list at least six behavioral traits characteristic of many gifted children?

2. What plan do I have for assessing individual strengths, weaknesses, and modes of learning for all the children in my room?

3. How do I accommodate the varying levels of ability in my class?

4. Can I list several means of differentiating curricular activities for bright and able youngsters?

5. Can I briefly describe a method I use for involving the bright and able youngster in planning and evaluating his/her own learning activities?

6. Can I list several ways gifted children are exposed to learning opportunities and experiences beyond the scope of my classroom?

7. How do I meet the affective needs of the gifted child?

Extending the Horizons of the Gifted By Utilizing Community Resources.

Students with outstanding ability or potential need opportunities which broaden their horizons and provide challenges. The school should assist teachers in planning experiences that extend the scope of activities beyond the confines of the classroom. Tangible help for classroom teachers stems from a school policy which:

— fosters an open atmosphere that encourages community involvement.

— promotes flexible scheduling that encourages extra-class activities.

— assists staff in developing and maintaining a community resource guide.

— values the adult mentor who serves as a role model and link to the world of careers.

— considers the library and museum to be a natural extension of the classroom.

— realizes that certain learning activities are best experienced in the natural environment, such as a wildlife refuge or an ocean laboratory.

—recognizes special talents of staff members and devises means to share their expertise within the school community.

— seeks parent cooperation and participation in exploring new avenues of experience for their gifted children.

Teachers are encouraged to plan activities for students that provide opportunities for exploring special interests. This is a basic ingredient in their development and growth toward independent, responsible behavior. This promotes career awareness and social skills through the interaction and exchange of ideas with peers and interested adults.

chapter 3

MEASURES USED TO ASSESS STUDENT NEEDS

Who Is the Gifted Child in My Classroom?

Ample time should be allowed during the first few weeks of the year for the children to become acquainted with you, the other children, and the learning environment. Your program should allow you time to observe the students and give them a period in which to adjust to routines, explore new materials and books, and get involved in learning. It should also provide direction and establish a sense of security as the children pursue learning activities. During this gradual introductory period, work with individuals and small groups and closely observe the students' behavior.

This may be accomplished by a simple chart or "plan of the day," with scheduled lessons, suggested activities, games, and projects. The amount of scheduled time will, of course, vary according to the individual preferences of the classroom teacher. This plan can be reviewed on a daily basis with the children making choices according to their needs, abilities, and interests.

Enrichment is a skilled tailoring of method and content in order to develop a curriculum suited to the individual needs of a particular gifted child. This requires first and foremost that the teacher know the child as an individual.

Prepare a folder for each child; gather background information from school records, special teachers, and other sources. To this, add work samples and notes gleaned from observations of individual behavior, interpersonal relationships, and group dynamics. Additional information may be extracted from tests administered during the first few weeks of school.

Standardized tests can help the teacher to analyze the child's performance in the classroom. An item analysis of achievement tests yields information about areas of strength and weakness. Any discrepancy between test performance and classroom behavior should be carefully studied. (For example, high standardized test scores coupled with low performance may indicate a lack of motivation attributable to insufficient challenge, emotional stress, or physical problems. On the other hand, low standardized test scores coupled with high performance may be caused by several factors, such as unfamiliarity with testing procedures and formats, a high level of anxiety, or a slow and methodical approach to tasks.)

There is no single criterion used in identifying the gifted child. A combination of both formal and informal measures from a variety of sources is deemed to be a valid approach. The observations of the classroom teacher are most certainly a significant factor in determining the child's needs and abilities.

Although some aspects of a child's development are best measured by objective tests or other standardized means, these measures do not present a complete picture of the child. It is important for teachers to regard the information yielded by standardized tests as clues for planning curriculum suited to an individual child's needs. They should not be misused as a way to sort children for ability grouping. As a teacher, you are in a unique position to sketch in all the subtle aspects of behavior that tests cannot capture. The children themselves present clues to their special needs and abilities by their actions in the classroom. An alert teacher is aware of the significance of observation in assessing a child's potential. Children whose innate abilities might otherwise go unnoticed, due to some special circumstances or disability, may be discoverd and nurtured by an alert teacher.

A teacher's chances of picking up behavioral clues from children with exceptional potential or ability are enhanced when:

1. the teacher is familiar with the behavioral characteristics of gifted children.
2. the teacher has a practical and systematic method for observing and recording behavior.
3. the teacher maintains a record of each child's progress on an ongoing basis.

A valid profile also includes observations of the child at play and in other social situations. Careful observation for a specific period of time increases the chance of assessing needs with a high degree of accuracy.

Gifted Child Behavioral Traits

The following forms are intended to assist you in identifying those children in your class who are gifted and require special educational strategies.

Behavioral Traits Guide (Form A)—research has indicated that many of these personality and behavioral traits have been demonstrated by gifted children. This list is, of course, only suggestive and is by no means intended to be inclusive. The gifted children in your class may possess some of these traits or may demonstrate other exceptional qualities of a different nature. This list is intended as an initial brief point of reference.

Observation Sheet (Form B)—provides a systematic method for observing and recording behavior. Please give thoughtful consideration to each child in your room.

The Individual Record Sheet (Form C)—may be kept in the child's cumulative folder to help the teacher maintain an ongoing record of progress. Teacher comments will prove helpful in assessing and planning a suitable program. Be sure to include work samples where possible.

FORM A
Gifted Child Behavioral Traits Guide

CURIOUS: keen observer; alert, inquisitive nature; questions the how and why of things; eager; pursues many interests in depth.

RAPID LEARNER: quickly masters facts; retains and applies information; needs minimal instruction on routine tasks.

SUSTAINS INVOLVEMENT: demonstrates persistent goal-directed behavior; has long attention span; ignores distractions; not easily discouraged by setbacks; self-motivated.

SOCIALLY AWARE: sensitive and intuitive; empathizes with others; flexible and open in manner; concerned with values and ideals.

ENJOYS READING: reads a wide range of materials for information and pleasure, including advanced selections; uses reference works effectively at an early age.

VERBAL PROFICIENCY: possesses an advanced vocabulary; expresses him or herself fluently; communicates precisely and accurately; expresses his or her own opinions freely; shows humor; asks probing questions.

RESPONSIBLE: works independently; needs minimal directions; understands and accepts guidelines; organizes tasks, peers, and events; often serves as a leader; respected by peers.

CRITICAL THINKING: analyzes and is logical; reasons out complicated things; evaluates situations; uses common sense; expresses and accepts constructive criticism.

CREATIVE: imaginative, versatile, and adaptable; flexible in ideas and actions; possesses problem-solving ability; original and inventive; gives clever and witty responses.

GENERALIZES: perceives and abstracts ideas; sees relationships; grasps underlying principles; makes valid assumptions about people, events, and things; integrates areas of knowledge.

SPECIAL ABILITY: possesses unusual interest and aptitude in an academic area; has exceptional mechanical ability; demonstrates talent or potential in one of the performing arts; sensitive to aesthetic quality and to the intrinsic beauty of things.

RESOURCEFUL: a producer who has a knack for using the limited resources, time, and people in a learning environment to achieve outstanding results; a prolific and creative author; his or her study and research results in original projects; generates new ideas and viewpoints; proposes novel solutions to peer conflicts.

Gifted Child Observation Sheet
Behavioral Traits

School_____

Teacher_____

Grade_____

Student's Names:
(Please check where out-
standing)

	Curious	Rapid Learner	Sustains Involvement	Socially Aware	Enjoys Reading	Verbal Proficiency	Responsible	Critical Thinking	Creative	Generalizes	Special Ability	Resourceful

Form C

Gifted Child – Behavioral Traits

Individual Record Sheet

Name _____   Date of Birth _____   School _____

Please indicated behavior by using the following
scale: (1) Low   (2) Average   (3) Outstanding

TRAITS	K	1	2	3	4	5	6
Curious							
Rapid Learner							
Sustains Involvement							
Socially Aware							
Enjoys Reading							
Verbal Proficiency							
Responsible							
Critical Thinking							
Creative							
Generalizes							
Special Ability							
Resourceful							

Grade 1 _____

Grade 2 _____

Grade 3 _____

Grade 4 _____

Grade 5 _____

Grade 6 _____

Teacher comments/remarks (special interests, content area
child excels in, unusual ability, talent, etc.)

Kindergarten _____

_____

_____

Establishing Natural Modes of the Gifted Child's Learning

A teacher has to be sensitive to a child's preferred learning modality. Learning modality means that sense—be it kinesthetic, visual, or aural—which acts as the major stimulus or influence in a child's ability to absorb external happenings in his/her learning process.

The child's preferred learning modality may be noted by carefully observing how the child gets involved in learning tasks. Teachers must teach to a child's sensory strengths. Some children are visual learners and learn best by seeing and reading. Auditory memory provides a foundation for youngsters who learn best by hearing. Kinesthetic learners use their bodies and manipulate objects as they rely on their senses to integrate learning experiences. While some children have a definite preferred modality strength, others have combined or mixed modality strengths. Many children learn by doing and at times combine kinesthetic involvement with other modalities. This enhances their ability to learn, retain, and apply information.

The classroom must provide many different experiences and materials for children to learn in the way that is most natural and functional for them. If a student has difficulty learning through any particular modality, the teacher needs to develop alternate strategies to adapt lessons and present information. This is crucial to the gifted child who may have a sensory impairment or a particular physical or learning disability.

The results of this information-gathering process may be easily recorded for each student in your class on a form such as **The Student Data Summary.** This will prove very helpful to you throughout the year whenever you plan for individual needs and monitor student progress.

Informal methods of data collection, may prove helpful to teachers when assessing the needs of children in their classrooms, including such things as a simple sociogram, **The Parent Information Letter**, and **The Student Interest Survey**.

Student Data Summary

Informal Classroom Record

Child's Name_____Birthdate_____Age_____Grade_____

School_____Teacher_____ Date_____

Preliminary Information

Tests/Background data_____ _____ _____ _____ Parents_____ _____ _____ Other_____ _____	General Observations_____ _____ _____ Child's Special Interests_____ _____ _____ Child's Learning Modality/Style_____ _____

Classroom Behavior

Academic Performance		Social Development	
Content Areas (list)	Comments	Behavioral Areas (list)	Comments

Summary

Areas of Strength/special ability_____ _____ Areas of special need_____	Recommendations/Plans_____ _____ Evaluation/Progress Review_____

Parents and Teachers as Partners

An understanding of the unique personality of the gifted child helps you to tailor a plan that suits individual student needs for a differentiated program.

A good rapport between parents and the teacher is essential in the elementary grades. After all, parents are a child's first teachers and are delighted when the curiosity and joy of learning are exhibited by their child. Parents are a rich source of information about the child's special needs, abilities, disabilities, and experiences. A form letter sent to the parents of all the children in your class will encourage them to respond and make it convenient for them to share information with you. This approach can help you identify and cultivate special talents and abilities that might otherwise go unnoticed.

Dear Parents,

Please take a few minutes to tell me about your child. This information will assist me in planning your child's instructional program. Feel free to include any additional comments or information.

I welcome any suggestions you may care to make concerning your child's special interests, needs, and abilities.

Thank you,

_____

(teacher)

(child's name) _____

1. Child's early development (walking, talking, reading, etc.)

_____

_____

2. Child's attitude toward learning and school (enthusiastic, reluctant, etc.)

_____

_____

3. Child's choice of friends (older, younger, prefers to play alone, etc.)

_____

4. Child's choice of play activities (prefers active games, builds things, etc.)

_____

_____

5. Child's reading habits (enjoys reading, seldom reads, etc.)

_____

_____

6. Child shows a talent or aptitude for (art, music, etc.)

_____

_____

7. Child's special interests (animals, collections, hobbies, etc.)

_____

_____

8. Child's attention span (sticks to a task, gets bored easily, etc.)

_____

_____

9. Child's imagination (pretends, creates dramatic play situations, etc.)

_____

_____

10. Child demonstrates curiosity (is inquisitive, wants to know the how and why of things, asks many questions, etc.)

_____

_____

11. Child's approach to tasks (rushes into, deliberate, etc.)

_____

_____

12. Child's special educational needs:

emotional _____

learning _____

physical _____

hearing _____

vision _____

health _____

Comments and additional information: _____

_____

_____

_____

_____

_____

Student Interest Survey

Knowing your students' interests opens new doors for interaction. Building on students' interests enhances learning and motivation. The student interest inventory is often a helpful aid for increasing your level of awareness in planning lessons, providing reading materials, and developing learning activities that will sustain involvement.

Informal methods are best for obtaining specific information in grades pre-K through 2. Information may be gleaned through individual and group discussion or by recording the child's choice of play and learning activities, noting items the child brings in for sharing time, and making anecdotal records and observations. Enjoy sharing and learning with the child.

Children are entitled to their otherness, as anyone is; and when we reach them, as we sometimes do, it is generally on a point of sheer delight, to us so astonishing, but to them so natural.

—Alastair Reid, *Places, Poems, Preoccupations*

STUDENT INTEREST SURVEY

Name _____ Grade _____ Date _____

What types of activities do you prefer? Please check the activities that interest you the most.

WRITING:

_____short stories
_____newspaper articles
_____special class reports
_____cartoons, riddles
_____crossword puzzles, anagrams, word games
_____poetry
_____plays, skits
_____diary or journal
other (please describe) _____

READING:

_____newspapers
_____magazines
_____reference books, atlases
_____textbooks
_____comics
_____books (circle favorite kinds—biography, science, history, adventure, sports, hobbies, religion, science fiction, fairy tales, geography, fiction,
other kinds _____)

SCIENCE:

_____working on a nature trail
_____doing experiments
_____working with animals
_____making things (circle favorite things—thermometer, compass, astrolabe, battery, solar heating unit, greenhouse, telescope, chick hatchery, ant farm, computer)

STUDYING:

_____chemistry
_____astronomy
_____nature, ecology
_____marine science
_____geology
other activity (please describe) _____

MATH:

_____making graphs (to measure team progress)
_____making up your own number system
_____learning about the stock market
_____solving difficult problems
_____working on problems with a calculator or a computer
_____puzzles, mazes, games of logic
other (please describe) _____

DRAMATICS:

_____acting in a play
_____directing a play
_____puppetry
_____pantomime
_____taking a course in filmmaking
_____acting in a radio broadcast
_____working on sets or a stage
other (please describe) _____

MUSIC:

_____learning about classical or folk music
_____making your own instrument
_____writing lyrics for songs
_____taking vocal lessons
_____learning to play an instrument
_____listening to music on the radio
_____attending (circle favorite) a concert, a rock festival, an opera, a jazz concert,
a piano recital, a ballet performance
_____singing in a chorus
_____composing music
_____taping and recording music
other _____

ART:

_____painting a mural on the school wall
_____learning to use watercolors
_____visiting a sculptor's studio
_____drawing cartoons
_____learning to weave
_____experimenting with ''junk'' art
_____visiting an art museum
_____modeling things out of clay
_____taking a mini-course on art history
other (please describe) _____

HOBBIES:

_____playing chess
_____photography
_____building models
_____playing with model trains
_____bird watching
_____cooking
_____hiking
_____owning a pet
other (please describe) _____
collections of (circle your interests) baseball cards, stamps, coins, old bottles, dolls, rocks,
postcards, other (please describe) _____

SPORTS:

_____ball games (circle your interests) football, baseball, tennis, basketball, soccer, other

_____swimming
_____skating: ice, roller
_____running
_____horseback riding
_____archery
_____hockey
other _____

I'd like to be a spectator at _____

Things I'd Like
Occupation you would like to learn more about?

_____

Field trip you would like to take?

_____

Subject you would like to learn more about?

_____

What do you like to do best when you are alone?

_____

What do you like to do best when you are with friends?

_____

Systematic Identification and Assessment

When a school district adopts a particular policy on the education of gifted pupils, it needs a comprehensive plan of action. Whether the focus is the regular classroom or other options, two elements must be present at the onset of the program.

The first is to establish a standard, flexible, nondiscriminatory district-wide process for the identification of gifted students. The second key item is the development of adequate evaluation procedures at the very onset of the program.

The following forms will help a school district provide a systematic approach for pupil identification and program planning. These forms incorporate ongoing evaluation procedures.

1. **Rating Scale Instruction Guide**

2. **Gifted Child Assessment Profile Record**

3. **Gifted Child Individual Education Plan Guide**

4. **Gifted Child Individual Education Plan Form**

5. **Individual Education Plan Supplementary Sheet—Provisions for Disabled Students**

RATING SCALE INSTRUCTION GUIDE
(A Model for General Identification Procedures)

School_____ Grade Levels_____ Date_____

<table>
<tr><td>The non-discriminatory assessment measures listed below are intended for use in the identification of gifted students. The rating scale and procedures established for use of these items will serve as a guide for assessment and program planning.</td><td>Initial Screening Process _____

_____

_____

_____</td></tr>
</table>

Identification and Assessment Measures

Items – Formal Testing	1. Below Average	2. Average	3. Above Average	4. Superior

Items – Informal Measures	Guidelines for Expanded Evaluation/Informal Measures

Supplementary Screening/Continuous Progress Evaluation_____

_____

_____

_____

_____

_____

Gifted Child Assessment Profile Record

It is essential to have a method for compiling assessment data and charting pupil progress. This enables effective identification of gifted students and assessment of individual needs. Criteria that designate a student as gifted should be established by the Committee prior to the identification process itself (e.g., I.Q. Tests, Achievement Tests, etc.). Guidelines for use of the rating scale should be specifically stated, because different school communities have divergent student populations and needs (e.g., an academic record of 90% might be considered (3.) ABOVE AVERAGE in one community while it might be considered (4.) SUPERIOR in another.

The RATING SCALE INSTRUCTION GUIDE can then serve as a model to the school district when the committee establishes guidelines for general identification procedures.

The cumulative ASSESSMENT PROFILE RECORD is helpful because it:

1) Provides information on how many children within a school district are gifted and in need of a differentiated program (usually 2 to 10% of the pupil population).

2) Highlights areas of giftedness of all grade levels so that administration and the committee know where special support services are needed.

3) Provides an equitable basis for establishing a cut-off point for certain program options such as resource room activities.

4) Provides a simple format for assessing and recording the widely divergent abilities of gifted students, and thus forms the basis for planning individual programs.

Since school districts do vary their guidelines, it will be up to the committee to establish specifics stating for whom this ASSESSMENT PROFILE RECORD will be maintained:

● Only those students identified as gifted (2 to 10% of the student population).
● Students who demonstrate academic ability or talent in a given area.
● Students who fall into the top 10 to 20% in achievement.
● All students within the district.

Name _____

Gifted Child
Assessment Profile Record

Date of Birth _____   School _____

*Identification/Assessment Measures
(Rating Scale: 1. low 2. average 3. above average 4. superior)

Grade Level	Item	Date	Rating	Item	Date	Rating	Item	Date	Rating	Item	Date	Rating	Item	Date	Rating	Assessment Summary
K																
1																
2																
3																
4																
5																
6																

Grade Level	Other Information	Program Adaptions (please specify special interest classes, tutor, etc.)	Comments/Recommendations
K			
1			
2			
3			
4			
5			
6			

*List all items (e.g. I.Q. Tests, Achievement Tests, Teacher Checklists, etc.) used in evaluative
procedure and rate according to established scale.

Preliminary Information
Gifted Child Individual Education Plan

The Individual Education Plan (IEP) is an assessment of the educational needs and abilities of gifted children, all of whom require differentiated programming and services from those normally provided by the regular school program. It focuses on individual development of unique abilities. This outlook encourages a diagnostic-prescriptive approach to the teaching/learning situation with ongoing assessment.

The instruments used for diagnosis by the classroom teacher may include:

checklists
readiness tests
standardized tests
informal tests
work samples
skills checklists
student interest inventories
I.Q. tests
information from parents
information from special staff
rating scales for gifted students

The results of these procedures are analyzed by the classroom teacher. After conferring with the student, special staff members and the administrator, a teacher draws up a preliminary program plan. It is important to hold a conference with the parents, who can provide valuable insights into the gifted child's background and interests. At this meeting early in the school year, teachers discuss goals and outline curriculum with parents. After discussing various aspects of the program, asking questions and viewing materials, parents have a better understanding of what their child's learning experiences will be. This enables the parents to extend and supplement the school program.

Parents may be given an opportunity to participate in activities when the need arises. They should be kept informed of their gifted child's progress; scheduled conferences, progress reports, meetings newsletters, school visitations and open houses can be used.

The teacher needs to meet with consultants, special educators, and the administrator to discuss the gifted child's special abilities, disabilities, and progress at regular intervals throughout the school year.

The child should be allowed to grow at his/her own rate. Each teacher must accommodate the curriculum—skills taught, content and method used and modality by which the child most readily learns—to the needs of each gifted child.

Individual Education Plan (IEP) Guide

The following information should be included:

1. an assessment of child's needs and list of measures used to evaluate them.
2. a summary of academic achievement and level of functioning.
3. a professional staff appraisal of work/study skills and social development.
4. special education and related services needed.
5. areas where acceleration or special training is advised.
6. long- and short-term goals and objectives for pupil development.
7. an outline and schedule of proposed differentiated learning activities which states methods and materials to be used.
8. a format for monitoring progress and maintaining an evaluation schedule.
9. input from the gifted pupil (where appropriate) regarding the setting of goals and program plans.
10. records of parent information, advisement and concurrence sought in development of a program plan.
11. outline of provisions for the physical education of a disabled student.
12. a list of the special services which will be provided for the disabled child, including:
    consultant services for the teacher;
    provisions for special materials;
    provisions for special equipment;
    special services for the child.

Gifted Child - Individual Education Plan

School_____

Name_____Grade_____ Date of Birth_____

Assessment of Needs - (evaluative procedure)_____

_____

_____

Academic Summary (present level of functioning)				
Rate (1) Low (2) Average (3) Outstanding				
Reading				
Language Arts				
Mathematics				
Science				
Social Studies				
Art				
Music				
Health				
Physical Ed.				
Other				

Behavioral Traits				
(✓) Check where outstanding				
Curious				
Rapid Learner				
Sustains Involvement				
Socially Aware				
Enjoys Reading				
Verbal Proficiency				
Responsible				
Critical Thinking				
Creative				
Generalizes				
Special Ability*				
Resourceful				

Teacher Comments:

Special areas of concern (physical, emotional or learning disability, developmental problem, content area weakness, etc.) See Supplementary Sheet _____

_____

*Special areas of talent or aptitude (present level of functioning)_____

_____

Recommended Pupil Development Plan (Differentiated Activities)

Social Growth

Objectives/Goals Long Range	Short Range	Program - Activities	Progress-Evaluation (specify method)

Work/Study Skills

Objectives/Goals Long Range	Short Range	Method - Materials	Progress-Evaluation (specify method)

Academic/Talent Areas

Objectives/Goals Long Range	Short Range	Method - Materials	Progress-Evaluation (specify method)

Conference Summary_____   Comments_____

_____   _____

_____   _____

_____   _____

_____   Signed_____

     Signed_____   (teacher)

          (student)   _____/_____

                        _____

                        (IEP Committee)

Progress Review Conference Dates (Teacher/IEP Committee)

_____   _____   _____   _____

Parent Comments_____

_____

Signed_____   Signed_____
           (parent)   (parent)

Scheduled Parent Conference Dates: _____   _____   _____   _____

The Gifted Child with a Disability

The concept of mainstreaming encourages teaching exceptional children in the least restrictive educational setting. If at all possible this means learning with their peers in a regular classroom. Classroom teachers must have adequate support services and practical information on how to adapt the learning environment to meet the emotional and educational needs of the exceptional child. Teachers should learn to view a child as an individual with a particular disability and never label the child by the handicap (e.g., deaf Martha).

While the philosophy of this book stresses the need for individualized education plans for all children, Public Law 94-142 mandates IEPs for children with a disability. If a disabled child who is gifted, is part of your class, a special educator should also be a member of the planning team developing an IEP. Steps eleven and twelve as listed in the IEP Guide are an integral part of the disabled child's individual education plan.

Special provisions for the child with a handicapping condition may be listed on the IEP Supplementary Sheet in order to state specific provisions in detail and to serve as a ready reference. You will be informed of special services which will be provided for the child (e.g., orientation and mobility for a visually handicapped child). Consultant services will be scheduled for you on a regular basis. Provisions for special materials and learning aides will be explained and demonstrated.

Once handicapped children have been identified as gifted or talented, decisions about educational placement are made to provide for an "appropriate" and "least restrictive" environment.

1. If you are considering placement in a regular classroom program for the gifted, the following questions may be considered.
    a. Does the child have the special skills needed to succeed (or compete with) those in the gifted grouping? Can alternative teacher resources be provided? For example, can consultation services be provided to a child who is developing skills?
    b. Does the child require medical or other special education services which could not be provided in the classroom gifted program? For example, does the child require the full-time teaching skills of a teacher for the emotionally disturbed?

    The child should not be excluded from a program "because s/he is handicapped," or because the school cannot provide for special education services (e.g., readers, specialized equipment, special education personnel time, adapted materials, reasonable curriculum and schedule adjustments) while the child is receiving education for the gifted. Ideally, the student should not be "deadlocked" in one placement because of his or her handicap. Individual needs and available resources must be considered. Alternative plans may have to be considered.
2. Independent of the placement decision, a team effort will be necessary to meet the continuing needs of the gifted-handicapped child. Only after a special education evaluation can decisions be made about the type and amount of services which will be needed.

Individual Education Plan - Supplementary Sheet
Provisions for Disabled Student

Name_____Grade_____ Date_____

Description of disability_____

_____

Statement of need for special services (present level of functioning)_____

_____

Physical Education

Goals-Objectives Long Range	Short Range	Program-Activities	Progress-Evaluation (specify method)

Special Instructional Materials/Methods

Goals-Objectives Long Range	Short Range	Format-Activities	Progress-Evaluation (specify method)

Special Equipment

Goals-Objectives Long Range	Short Range	Format-Activities	Progress-Evaluation (specify method)

Comments/Remarks_____   Teacher consultation schedule:

_____   _____ _____

    Signed_____   _____ _____
          (Special educator)   _____

        _____   Signed_____
                               (Classroom teacher)
        _____
            (IEP Committee members)

Comments/Remarks:_____

Signed_____   Signed_____
              (Parent)   (Parent)

WEAVING A WEB OF ENRICHMENT FOR PRIMARY GIFTED CHILDREN

chapter 4

The Learning Process in the Primary Grades

A teacher cannot impart learning to young students. What can a teacher do? What is a teacher's role? If a child's learning is based on experiences, the teacher must then become a facilitator or guide for these learning experiences.

In diagnosing and planning for a child's needs, consideration must be given to the whole child and his/her intellectual, emotional, and physical development. In preparing the learning environment care must be taken to provide the opportunity to interact with peers as well as explore, perform, question, manipulate, and discuss.

When adapting lessons for the gifted child, certain modes of thinking should be stressed:
1. higher levels of cognition
2. creativity
3. problem finding and solving

How is the gifted child's growth best served? Emphasis is placed on a child-oriented approach which considers the individual as the basis for organization. A child must be able to progress at his/her own rate and pattern. According to Piaget's theories, the learning process is developmental. Teaching abstract concepts to primary children is of dubious value unless based on concrete experiences. Receptive learning is often difficult even for bright children because it involves understanding verbal constructs and relating these constructs to existing cognitive structure.

Young children naturally demonstrate an eagerness to learn by doing, and both Dewey and Montessori placed great emphasis on this aspect of behavior. Conceptual growth is best served by direct experience and the discovery approach. In this way a child sustains motivation as learning satisfies both curiosity and a growing need for independence.

An intense involvement by the youngster is needed to develop the receptive, expressive, and associative abilities so crucial to the learning process. Being actively involved in the process enhances retention and aids the child in the transfer of this learning in a productive, functional way. This also facilitates creativity and divergent thinking in children.

Emphasis should be placed on the learning process itself and on an active output by the youngster. By becoming a producer in learning experiences, the child grows in self-concept and is encouraged toward independent behavior.

Teachers must deal effectively with THE THREE C's OF LEARNING in order to plan a responsive and challenging classroom environment for the gifted child.

THE THREE C'S OF LEARNING

CARING - Affective Needs
The teacher must be aware of the child's maturational and emotional needs and offer the warm

support and guidance that promotes a healthy self-concept and acceptance of others. Sensitivity to and awareness of the behavioral traits common to many gifted children are important parts of this acceptance and understanding.

CONDITIONS - Learning Environment

The teacher must possess a knowledge of the individual needs, abilities, and disabilities of each child and how that child learns best. Only then can the teacher decide how and when to set up a variety of activities and materials for the child's emotional, intellectual, and social development.

CURRICULUM - Cognitive Needs

The teacher must know specific strategies in curriculum design for the gifted and various approaches to differentiated curriculum. Opportunities must be created for the child to produce and learn in an atmosphere that is intellectually challenging and personally rewarding.

Some Suggestions for Teachers of Gifted Children in the Primary Grades

Teachers of gifted children in the primary grades should be highly skilled in the following roles:
  observing behavior
  planning learning experiences
  extending concepts and vocabulary
  guiding developmental needs

The teacher of gifted primary students must listen and be sensitive to the child's sense of wonder and curiosity. An observant teacher tunes in to the child's questions during learning and play experiences; those questions indicate what has captured his/her imagination and "the need to know." Through play, young children learn and make sense of the world around them.

Leadership may be demonstrated in the primary grades by the creative child who says "Let's" and turns the playground into a spaceship or the sand table into a busy dock. A bright child often leads classmates in a serial play experience which is created and elaborated upon over a period of days. The puppets may become Columbus and his crew. Interest then wanes but may be revived at a later date as new information is received and assimilated through play experiences. Through the social aspects of play, concepts are slowly developed as the child communicates, integrates, and extends newly acquired information and vocabulary.

Often children engage in dramatic play after taking a trip, viewing a puppet show or film, or hearing a story that captures their imagination. An alert teacher observes and listens to the children in order to determine whether or not they accurately understand events or concepts. The teacher must be sensitive and clarify concepts and points of confusion as the need arises. The gifted child needs help in developing a conceptual framework to organize information and extend meanings.

If a teacher is to guide a young child's intellectual development, there must be an awareness of the child's readiness for different kinds of learning experiences.

The teacher of a young gifted child needs to accept this child as the child is and understand that behavior ranges from a startling maturity and grasp of concepts to the more typical immaturity and egocentrism. Therefore, one should not be surprised when, for example, a child who shows keen insight into complicated social problems pushes or hits another child for breaking his purple crayon.

Children tend to develop unevenly, and gifted children are usually no exception to this rule. This factor is important to keep in mind when assessing children's social and developmental needs as well as their academic skills. Certain children may excel in reading or math but may be upset because they are unable to tie their sneakers for gym or skip a rope.

Developing a positive self-image is important for gifted children, who require support and guidance from their teacher. These children often set high standards for themselves and become frustrated and upset when they do not readily achieve them.

As you plan the learning environment, pay attention to the physical set-up as well as to the materials and resources. Activities that foster learning independence and creativity should encourage freedom in the use of materials and resources. For young gifted children, there should be an abundance of activities that promote learning through the senses.

Plan experiences for the kinesthetic development of gifted primary students through music, drama, and creative movement. If you do not feel confident about your ability to provide a good music program, use supplementary materials such as Ruth Spencer's *Early Childhood Music Kit* (see The Bibliography). Since children learn by doing, include concrete experiences that involve them and provide intellectual stimulation through inquiry and discovery learning.

The wise teacher capitalizes on the interests that children bring with them to school. Tried and true routines such as show and tell or similar sharing activities can be creatively adapted by the teacher to encourage children to reveal their special interests and develop their communications skills. This serves as a springboard for concept development and vocabulary building.

Through sharing routines and the like, the child learns how to accurately relate an event or describe an object and how to interact with peers by answering their questions. The child gains in group communication skills as s/he quickly learns to speak clearly and concisely in order to hold the interest of classmates.

Remember to be attentive and respectful of children's thoughts and ideas. Do not talk down to them; use adult vocabulary. Encourage the development of precise listening skills and the ability to follow complicated oral directions.

Many gifted children already know how to read when they enter school and great care must be taken to provide a good reading program to meet their special needs. The teacher should be aware that young gifted children cannot spend most of their reading time alone, even with interesting books and lessons. It is not reading materials on an appropriate level that make a reading program suitable for a particular gifted child.

Rather, it is personal attention, frequent interaction, and nurturing support from the teacher that provide a reading program of quality.

As with many other young children, gifted children often express their thoughts verbally and tend to think out loud. Challenging reading materials often pose stimulating problems and unleash a barrage of questions to answer, concepts to discuss, ideas to share, and values to clarify. The teacher cannot assume that the children understand advanced reading materials. Artful discussion and questioning reveals the child's grasp of vocabulary and allows the teacher to clarify or extend meanings.

The teacher may develop alternate plans for instruction, such as an individualized reading program which could utilize cluster grouping for the direct teaching of reading skills. The gifted primary child needs careful instruction in word-analysis techniques, in varying his/her rate of reading, and in a myriad of related reading skills.

Don't isolate the primary gifted child; s/he needs to be part of a group and often thrives on social interaction. Children, regardless of ability level, need direct instruction when certain fundamental language skills are introduced and taught. Remember, however, that gifted children rarely need endless drill and boring workbook pages for skills mastery.

The classroom teacher should seek the support of resource people such as the reading specialist and librarian in meeting the needs of gifted primary children.

Gifted primary students are often intrigued by a language-experience approach to reading and writing. This method builds on the children's experiences and encourages interests. It is compatible with the need to develop language in an interesting, personalized manner. Children should have an opportunity to practice skills creatively. They enjoy seeing other children select stories to read, and this motivates budding authors.

A sensitive teacher can assist gifted children in developing social skills by providing many opportunities to interact with peers. Gifted children may have adjustment problems, such as shyness and a tendency to be bossy or too talkative, and they need warm encouragement in developing positive social behavior and attitudes. The teaching/learning environment should promote children's acceptance of themselves and others. Gifted children are often socially aware and readily perceive differences in others.

There are many intellectual challenges involved in the socialization process of young children. Gifted children are usually sensitive and readily discern what is appropriate behavior. They must learn to interact with peers, share, deal with aggression, give and receive affection, accept the differences of others, and learn to cope with group demands. Gifted primary children want and need opportunities to discuss rules and problems and not simply conform to the do's and don'ts of the classroom. They should develop and clarify their own values and understandings.

Young children learn to understand and appreciate our democratic way of life through early classroom experiences and practice these democratic values on a day-to-day basis. They need support and guidance in understanding their needs and accepting their gifted and non-gifted classmates who may have physical handicaps or other limitations. An understanding of friendship, responsible behavior, concern for the rights of others, and an openness and respect for the ideas and backgrounds of peers are concepts that children experience and develop in the classroom.

Gifted primary education, while child centered, does not negate the importance of learning facts and mastering fundamental processes. The children may explore fundamental concepts from science and other areas in a manner in which basic understandings can be acquired through concrete experiences. They can use their senses as they observe and classify and make generalizations in the process of concept formation. Their intellectual curiosity is stimulated, and they are eager to determine the how's and why's of many things in the environment. Provide the children with opportunities to associate ideas, test hypotheses, and work on cause-and-effect relationships. As a result, they are able to learn how to interpret data and reach logical conclusions.

Gifted children often finish routine tasks in a skillful manner and appear at their teacher's desk with the plea, "What can I do next?" Their boundless energy and enthusiasm for learning require experiences which actively engage them in creative problem-solving activities with a minimum of adult supervision.

Since the teacher wishes to furnish extended opportunities to acquire information and understanding, adding horizontal enrichment (more activities on the same level of difficulty) merely to fill in the school day is not a defensible procedure. If gifted children are going to be challenged, the teacher should provide more valuable activities which allow them to develop concepts and higher-level thought processes—thought igniters, not boring drills.

Activity centers that sustain involvement through concrete experiences are well suited to this purpose. These allow children to assimilate and master fundamental concepts a little bit at a time.

Planning an experience-centered curriculum that promotes cognitive growth and stimulates creativity is only a preliminary step for the teacher. The focus must be on assessing and guiding the developmental needs of young gifted children. The basic need for security and independence, common to all children, is certainly shared by gifted children. However, due to their advanced skills mastery and rapid grasp of ideas, they are often expected to become self-directed learners prematurely. The teacher must assess each child's level of maturity and ability to function independently. These early efforts must be initiated with care in order to avoid anxiety and

Today's date is _____

OPEN CLASS

| READING GROUPS | READING SKILLS BOX | LISTENING TAPES |

| MATH | INDEPENDENT ACTIVITIES | |

| SCIENCE | SPECIAL PROJECTS | CONFERENCES |

MUSIC

| SOCIAL STUDIES | GROUP WORK | CREATIVE WRITING |

SHOW & TELL
ACTIVITY CARDS

frustration on the part of the child. Help the child plan goals and organize his/her day in a sequential manner. Develop a simple routine for helping the child to evaluate his/her progress.

Many advantages flow from involving the children in the development of daily plans. Each child gets the security of knowing where he/she fits in and does not feel left out or isolated. Each youngster is better able to understand behavioral expectations and his/her responsibility in class, small group, and individual learning situations. Also, an overview of the progression of activities helps each to anticipate and adapt to changing situations and expectations.

Remember that gifted children often become so involved in a particular task that they are reluctant to stop in order to participate in a group activity such as gym or music. A gentle reminder about an event prior to the scheduled time makes adjustment easier.

Advanced skills and concept formation are not the only criteria for self-directed learning experiences. Avoid applying pressure to perform and try to promote independent learning in a manner that provides a sense of self-direction without stress.

Avail yourself of any support services, such as those provided by parent volunteers, student mentors, or other special staff (including people who perform psychological and guidance services, special educators of the disabled and emotionally disturbed, and learning consultants). This provides frequent, warm interaction on a more personalized basis for the youngsters.

This program for gifted primary children is unique because in most instances they do not have the prerequisite skills to attempt a simple research project without help from their teacher each step of the way. As a facilitator of learning experiences, the teacher extends opportunities for children to acquire information about special interests and about things in the environment that arouse their curiosity.

Young children pursuing independent learning need help in research and in devising ways of sharing thoughts, ideas, and information. They grow in awareness and understanding of these skills and processes through many experiences. Consider the example of a child who is interested in fish, is delighted with the science books, and spends much time poring over pictures of fish. Noting the child's involvement, the teacher helps the youngster select several books about fish in the school library while introducing the child to the use of the card catalog. The child discovers that these specialized books not only have more detailed information, but also an abundance of colorful illustrations. The child could also look at the aquarium in another classroom. This experience provides first-hand information through observation and discussion with the students who are taking care of the fish. As a follow-up activity, the parents may wish to take the child to an aquarium or pet store. Next, the youngster needs help in recording and organizing the information and in selecting a method of sharing the results. The latter may take the form of a simple picture story or an experience chart.

Young children are frequently expected to write a report about their early attempts at research. Children confronted with this task often become frustrated because their grasp of concepts may exceed their ability to communicate in writing. Gifted youngsters should not be pushed to write before they are ready. Writing develops as abstractive, physical, and other abilities develop. To help the children achieve expressive fluency, the teacher can assist them in developing other means of communicating and sharing ideas and information.

Start with simple, direct experiences and progress to abstract methods of reporting and sharing information. Show-and-tell effectively demonstrates a child's thoughts and ideas in a simple, concrete way. As a child develops the ability to assimilate and share knowledge, s/he usually progresses to representation (for example, setting up a model of an airport, dioramas, puppets, etc.). Finally, the child can produce a written report, graph, or chart which conveys his/her messages in an abstract manner.

Continue to read aloud to gifted children even though they may be adept at reading. Besides being an enjoyable experience, listening to stories provides children with a sense of the rhythm and patterns of spoken language. Expressive, fluent language sustains involvement as it expands vocabulary and the children's fund of general knowledge. Bright children's listening comprehension often far exceeds their ability to grasp meaning from the printed page.

Gifted children usually have advanced vocabularies and are often fascinated by words. Many enjoy word play. Puns and limericks delight them. Be sure to include in your reading classics such as *Alice in Wonderland* and *Through the Looking Glass*. Edward Lear's *A Book of Nonsense* and *The Wonderful O* by James Thurber stir the imagination as well as enhance vocabulary. Myths, fables, and biographies continue to hold a place of honor on the bookshelves of children of all ages. Sparkling, fresh poetry improves and cultivates a child's sensitivity for the imagery, aesthetics, and beauty of language.

Don't discount the value of a picture file. The visual appeal provided by photographs, picture books, art prints, and magazine pictures continues to be important for all primary children, including the gifted. Pictures stimulate a child's imagination and provide a focal point for expressive language development.

Reliance on reading as the main source of data gathering may prove to be frustrating. The ability to comprehend facts often surpasses skills in coping with the difficult format of some textbooks. The use of a wide variety of media, resources, and experiences allows a youngster to expand concepts and reasoning ability while developing process skills.

Parents are an important part of early childhood education. Try to involve parents in a conference session early in the school year. Assess their child's needs and explore program goals and plans with them. During a child's primary years, parents often need support in realizing that their role and relationship with their child is changing in new, exciting, and wonderful ways. Their child is taking his/her first steps on the road to learning as a unique and independent scholar.

Support parental efforts which encourage the growth of the child toward independence and simultaneously maintain family bonds of security, love, and guidance. Share information about class events and the child's progress. This enables parents to extend classroom activities. This open approach should do much to relieve the anxiety of those parents who may otherwise tend to become too directly involved in their child's learning experiences. Tact and skillful diplomacy are sometimes required of a teacher in order to help parents avoid becoming overly concerned and to encourage a healthy interest in and support for their child's endeavors.

Stress the importance of balancing creative endeavors and the development of the intellect with time for friends, relaxation, and physical activity—just for the fun of it.

When conferring with parents and evaluating the progress of their youngster, let them know you care for their child in a warm and personal way. Encourage their input and comments. They can help at home. Discuss community resources they can use to help enrich their child's life—for example, the public library and other institutions are excellent resources for parents of the gifted. Have information available about the hours and programs of local museums and libraries. (Many libraries and museums have this information printed on leaflets, which you can distribute to parents.) Also, suggest reading lists for enrichment and supplementary reading that tie in with your program. Remember, parents are a child's first teachers, and they delight in the curiosity and joy of learning exhibited by their child. Moreover, parent volunteers can do much to extend and enrich the scope of your program.

Some points for teachers to remember:
1. A program for gifted primary students should not be merely a diluted version of activities adapted from the upper elementary program. Rather, the primary program must respond to the unique social, emotional, and developmental needs of young gifted children. These needs form the basis for organizing differentiated learning experiences that stimulate intellectual growth.

2. The teacher can organize learning experiences which:
   assess needs
   promote cognitive growth
   meet affective needs
   support social growth
   develop concepts
   expand vocabulary
   encourage creativity
   guide thinking skills
   promote interaction between home and school

Primary Grades: A Thematic Approach To Learning

A practical way to organize learning experiences for primary-grade children is to take a thematic approach to teaching. Content is not the primary focus; rather, emphasis is placed on processes and expansion of basic skills. Activities are differentiated according to children's ability in any given area.

Young gifted children require a curriculum that reflects their unique abilities and potential. A curriculum that interrelates all subjects allows for meaningful learning experiences. A well-structured curriculum for the gifted provides for creative and innovative practice in all areas of skills development.

The theme can be divided into learning modules. Depending on the interests of the children, these modular learning units can:
   be related to their special interests
   allow for a more in-depth approach that is deemed valuable for the gifted.

When designing a module related to the theme, consider the children's interests and available resources. Integrate basic reading and math skills, scientific concepts, social studies, art, music, and other areas around the theme. The interrelated curriculum allows children to apply and practice skills in a meaningful way. They learn to think precisely and logically. Math should not be confined to workbook pages but ought to be related to learning activities as the children measure, tabulate, and apply skills in a functional way.

Young children are inquisitive about the sights, sounds, and smells of things in their environment. They want to look, touch, and ask endless questions in order to satisfy their curiosity. Concepts are built through experiences which allow the child to see relationships, classify, discriminate, and generalize.

In the primary grades, data is not emphasized. Content is considered a channel through which children learn to master thinking and learning skills. Early mastery and expansion of the basic tools of learning is important for gifted children who are eager and curious to learn on their own.

Bloom's taxonomy can serve as a guide for planning lessons that will aid in developing higher-level thought processes.

Children become motivated and enthusiastic when a topic is presented in an interesting way. The teacher, aware of the numerous resources available, may introduce an idea related to a current theme; or a child may bring in for sharing time an item that is related to classroom study. This item of special interest provides the cue for developing a theme-related learning module that children can help plan.

A good way to organize thoughts, ideas, and questions into appropriate learning activities is to work with the children to develop a simple flow chart in the form of a learning web. This web need not be completed at once but may be added to as the youngsters' needs, abilities, and interests suggest new directions for learning.

As the children get involved in the flow chart, they learn classifying and outlining skills. As an added bonus, the chart can serve as a point of reference for evaluation, review, and reinforcement of concepts.

Before developing a learning web with the children, make sure that:
- the topic ties in with the general theme and curriculum.
- it relates to the varying needs, abilities, and concerns of the children.
- learning activities can be developed which encourage personal growth and positive values.
- the theme offers opportunities to expand basic skills in creative and innovative ways.
- the theme encourages the children to develop higher-level thought processes.
- resources, materials, and first-hand experiences are readily available in order that the topic may be pursued in depth.

The degree of the children's involvement in planning learning activities will, of course, vary according to their level of maturity. Use the following simple steps. The process may take several days, depending upon the ability of the group to sustain involvement.

1. List the topic on a large sheet of paper taped to the blackboard.
2. Encourage the children to brainstorm and call out ideas related to the topic. Record their ideas.
3. Plan a learning web by grouping related areas.
4. Work with the children to develop a list of questions.
5. Use Bloom's Taxonomy, the learning web, and questions to help plan learning activities on different levels.
6. Develop a list of resources, materials, resource people, and related trips. Encourage suggestions from children.
7. Have the children select topics they wish to explore.
8. Plan for sharing and evaluation.

Planning with the children gives them direction and purpose, fosters goal-oriented behavior, and develops oral expression. They learn to value their own thoughts and the ideas of others.

Many factors determine how the teacher structures learning experiences. When planning, keep the traits of each gifted child—skill in reading advanced materials, ability to sustain involvement, etc.—in mind and use this as a rationale for structuring specific activities. You must become skilled at matching each child with appropriate tasks and materials. Learning must fit the child.

Be sure to consider modality for learning and provide open-ended experiences. Gifted children must be challenged and at times should be grouped to work with peers of similar ability. A word of caution is in order, however, because gifted children need to interact in various groupings. It is illogical to assume that a gifted child is only having a worthwhile learning experience when working with advanced peers. Children work and play together for many reasons:

special interests
ability
friendship
tasks

Help gifted children develop leadership ability within the social structure of the class. When not exposed to constant ability grouping, they will learn to achieve emotional and social rapport with many different youngsters.

The activities suggested by the learning web can be incorporated within the framework of a learning center. This flexible approach encourages peer interaction and accommodates a wide range of abilities in the primary grades. Learning center experiences encourage children to relate ideas and try things out for themselves.

Centers vary in structure and form and can readily be adapted to many types of classrooms. Planning a center that meets divergent student needs involves more than assembling a random assortment of clever theme-related activities to keep children occupied. The goals of a detailed curriculum plan for a learning center are to:

- encourage learning by doing and process-oriented education.
- promote open-ended, student-selected activities.
- provide a wide variety of materials and resources on different ability levels.
- extend opportunities to engage in problem-solving experiences.
- expand the knowledge that children assimilate and extend concepts related to the theme.
- foster social development by encouraging positive habits and attitudes.
- improve and expand thinking and learning skills.
- provide opportunities for creative behavior.
- employ multi-sensory approaches to learning.
- provide opportunities for product development, sharing, and evaluation by the child.

Keep the learning center simple. Avoid excessive use of elaborate and often distracting decorations. Whenever possible, use real objects and accurate reproductions (e.g., a detailed bird photo instead of a cute cartoon).

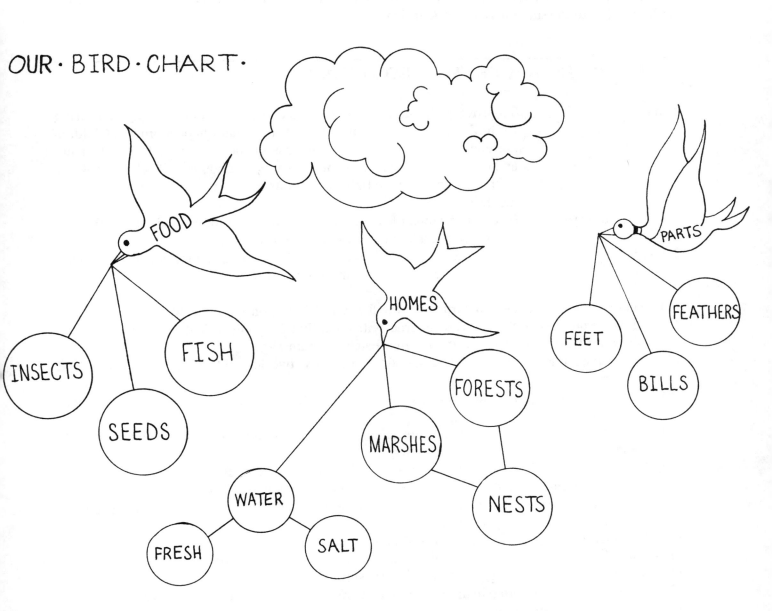

OUR · BIRD · CHART ·

FOOD
INSECTS
FISH
SEEDS

HOMES
FORESTS
MARSHES
NESTS
WATER
FRESH
SALT

PARTS
FEET
FEATHERS
BILLS

THEME: WHAT ABOUT ANIMALS (Grades K-3)

The following module on birds is developed from the theme **WHAT ABOUT ANIMALS?** and shows ways to differentiate learning activities using Bloom's Taxonomy as a guide. These initial experiences encourage primary children to develop the problem-solving abilities and study skills needed to pursue independent learning.

MODULE: OUR FEATHERED FRIENDS

Purpose: To provide children with first-hand experiences in observing and caring for birds, and thus awaken an interest in all natural phenomena. Children are encouraged to grow in awareness of the delicate balance of nature and develop an appreciation of its beauty and bounty. This helps provide a foundation for a lifetime of responsible stewardship for the environment.

General Concept: Birds are friends of man, yet many birds are threatened with extinction due to man-made changes in the environment.

Knowledge: In order to exercise higher levels of cognition, children need to acquire a data base comprised of the following facts:

(1) There are many species of birds all over the world living on land and water.
(2) Birds are interdependent with and interact with other living organisms in the environment.
(3) Birds are warm-blooded vertebrates that hatch from an egg.
(4) Birds share many common characteristics: two eyes, two legs, a bill or beak, wings, and feathers.
(5) Birds vary greatly in color, some sporting bright plumage and others blending into their surrounding habitat.
(6) Birds vary greatly in size. Some are small like the hummingbird, while others, like the eagle, are very large.
(7) Birds have long, hollow, lightweight bones that allow air to pass through.
(8) Birds communicate with each other through body movements, songs, and calls.
(9) Birds eat a great deal for their size. Foods vary according to the kind of bird and may include insects, berries, small animals, fish, and seeds.
(10) You can tell what type of food a bird eats by the shape of its beak.
(11) Sometimes people feed birds in the winter, when food is difficult to obtain.
(12) Some species of birds migrate instinctively in summer and winter along north-south flyways.
(13) The bird found most often in the cities is a hardy member of the dove family called the pigeon.
(14) Birds mate and build nests and take care of their young. Baby birds grow to resemble their parents.
(15) Some baby birds such as turkeys, ducklings, and chicks require less care when they are young because they are mobile.
(16) Birds without feathers are usually helpless at birth and need lots of care from their parents.
(17) Eggs of various birds are different sizes and colors and may hatch anywhere from 14 to 23 days.
(18) Some birds build their nests in trees, but many birds build their nests in other places.
(19) People who build birdhouses must take care to build them in places not readily accessible

to cats and other animals.

(20) Wild game and domestic fowl serve as a rich source of food for people.

(21) Ornithologists are scientists who study birds.

(22) There are organized groups dedicated to preserving birds and other wildlife.

(23) We need national and state bird sanctuaries to prevent certain natural habitats from being destroyed.

(24) The use of chemical and poisonous insecticides must be regulated by law.

(25) We must protect our forests, marshes, and wetlands from wanton destruction.

(26) Hunters and sportsmen need to obtain a license and observe certain regulations.

(27) We must all learn more about protection if we are to help preserve the environment and save birds threatened with extinction.

Skills Development:

Children reinforce and develop skills as they engage in the following experiences. They . . .

- learn to use their sense of hearing with increased sensitivity and awareness as they listen to environmental sounds.
- learn to recognize and classify sounds as they listen to bird calls.
- profit by visiting a special habitat (zoo, park, bird sanctuary, or other designated environment) and gather information and facts.
- learn to follow directions and apply math skills as they construct a simple birdhouse.
- develop the ability to make generalizations about the similarities and differences of various species of birds.
- develop the ability to relate and apply concepts as they work with the chick hatchery (or other such project).
- engage in problem solving experiences as they plan, choose, arrange, construct and evaluate information and materials for various activities and projects.
- learn to observe and record seasonal changes in the environment and relate this to bird behavior.
- learn to recognize and name a variety of shrubs, bushes and trees as habitats for certain species of birds.
- learn to use maps and apply directional terms by tracing the north-south flyways of migrating birds.
- develop facility in reading to answer questions and gather facts from a wide variety of sources.
- learn to acquire information about special interest topics by writing letters.
- reinforce and expand writing ability by preparing reports, stories and other projects.
- assume responsibility for maintaining materials, projects, work space and equipment in good order.
- participate in group discussion, planning and work projects in a cooperative manner.
- develop visual acuity in recognizing and naming various species of birds.
- practice using special tools, equipment and materials to obtain information and develop projects.
- develop an awareness of birds in our cultural heritage (both in fact and fantasy) through literature, nursery rhymes, poetry and other sources.
- use a chart or other recording device to evaluate the growth and behavioral patterns of the chicks they are caring for in the science center.
- select and choose a method for sharing the results of their experiences in a creative summary.

Values and Attitudes:

It is hoped that these learning activities will promote self-reliance and skills mastery to the degree that the gifted child will experience joy in learning. Gains in self-concept will enable the youngster to cope more successfully with a variety of emotional, social, and intellectual demands.

Helping a child discover the wonder of natural phenomena may instill a respect and reverence for all life.

Evaluation:

The teacher's observations and estimate of concepts learned and skills mastered should be evaluated on an individual basis. Informal tests may be developed and student performance in various activities may be evaluated and recorded by the teacher.

Using Bloom's Taxonomy To Guide Primary Learning Experiences

KNOWLEDGE

finding out
observing
data gathering
Observe and record bird behavior. Make a file of bird facts and vocabulary words. Read to gather information. Listen to people. Ask questions.

COMPREHENSION

explain
recall
describe
Play the game CAN YOU GUESS MY SECRET? How can you tell what I like to eat by the shape of my beak? Can you describe my air conditioning system? How are my bones different from the bones of other animals?

APPLICATION

use data
operate
model
Validate information received by building a bird feeder. Put suet, crumbs and seeds out. Observe birds at feeder. What birds come? How do they behave? Draw a picture of what you see.

ANALYSIS

classify
investigate
compare
Make a bird chart. Choose a way to classify types of birds:
    environment
    shapes of beaks
    size of bird
    nesting habits
    kinds of food
    migrating and non-migrating

SYNTHESIS

imagine
design
adapt
Make a mural about birds. Make up some riddles about birds. Make up a bird dance.

EVALUATION

justify choices
decide
prove
Is it a good bird for a pet? Is it a good house for this bird? Why? Are you a good pet owner for a bird? Make a book on bird care for pet owners.

Knowledge

Introduce entry-level learning experiences: discovering, finding out, gathering information, exploring key concepts. Establishing an adequate data base is essential in the primary grades. A broad variety of experiences on LEVEL I—KNOWLEDGE are described in detail. This may demonstrate ways to expand and develop activities on all levels. A series of activities on this level will follow.

#1 SKILLS:
- reinforce and expand learning through the senses.
- Develop the ability to sustain involvement.
- Build upon prior learning experiences as child develops the ability to recall and recognize various items.

MATERIALS/RESOURCES:
Motivation cues consisting of various objects related to birds.

ACTIVITIES:
The teacher facilitates involvement and encourages motivation by discussing key concepts and presenting objects related to birds. The children are given opportunities to view and manipulate items such as nests, eggs, feathers, bird seed, bones, charts, pictures and models. Listening to

EARLY CHILDHOOD
BLOOM'S TAXONOMY

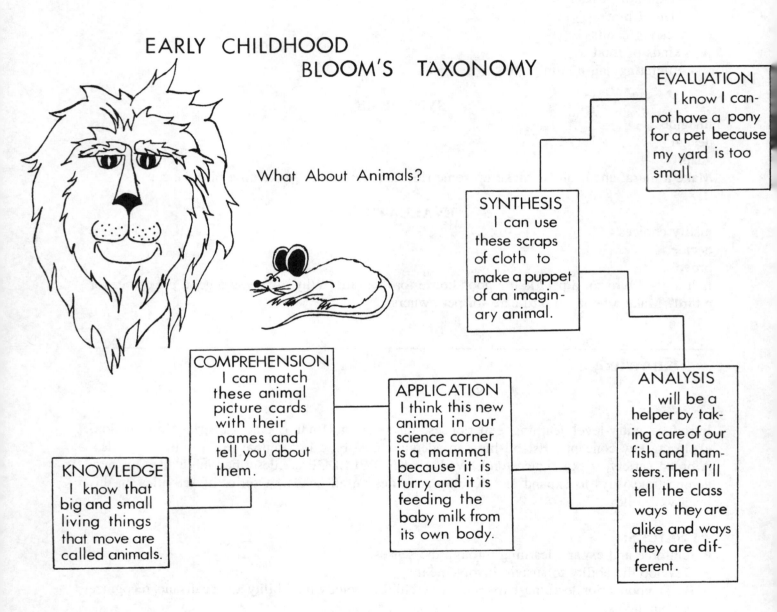

What About Animals?

EVALUATION
I know I cannot have a pony for a pet because my yard is too small.

SYNTHESIS
I can use these scraps of cloth to make a puppet of an imaginary animal.

COMPREHENSION
I can match these animal picture cards with their names and tell you about them.

APPLICATION
I think this new animal in our science corner is a mammal because it is furry and it is feeding the baby milk from its own body.

ANALYSIS
I will be a helper by taking care of our fish and hamsters. Then I'll tell the class ways they are alike and ways they are different.

KNOWLEDGE
I know that big and small living things that move are called animals.

tapes and records of bird sounds and calls provides an intriguing learning experience. Throughout this exploratory process children are encouraged to discuss their own experiences and ask questions.

#2 SKILLS:
- Gather and retain information from viewing and listening to a filmstrip.
- Clarify and expand basic understandings.
- Develop an ability in oral language through questions and group discussion.

MATERIALS/RESOURCES:
Filmstrip on bird behavior.

ACTIVITIES:
The children listen to and view a filmstrip and gather information about:
>   birds nesting
>   birds hatching
>   young birds
>   feeding and care
>   growth and change

The children then ask questions. Ample opportunity must be provided for group discussion. In this way children learn not only to express their own thoughts but to listen to and value the ideas of others.

#3 SKILLS:
- Learn to participate in a brainstorming session.
- Focus on a concept and ask relevant questions.
- Learn how to plan and outline a flow chart to guide study activities.
- Select and choose appropriate resources for learning activities.

MATERIALS/RESOURCES:
Chart paper or two large sheets of newspaper; marking pen.

ACTIVITIES:
Brainstorm with your students and record their ideas on chart paper. Plan a learning web which organizes related ideas.

Develop a list of questions with the children. Include provocative questions of your own to stimulate interest and develop concepts:
>   Do all birds build nests?
>   How do birds learn to fly?
>   How do the babies get out of their shell?

List resources, materials and learning activities that may help solve some problems and answer questions. Guide children in planning and selecting activities for learning. Set up and structure materials and resources for a learning center, task cards, special projects, etc.

#4 SKILLS:
- Use senses to explore a natural habitat and acquire information.
- Make first-hand observations of bird behavior.
- Use special equipment such as field glasses and bird guide book.

MATERIALS / RESOURCES:
Plan a trip that allows children to observe birds in their natural habitat. Places to visit may include: a neighborhood walk, nature trail, zoo, aviary, park, wildlife refuge, etc.

ACTIVITIES:
Involve the children in planning the trip and discuss possibilities for learning activities. Provide clues that will enhance the children's ability to learn by listening and observing. Suggest sounds and calls to listen for. Acquaint them with trees, shrubs and bushes that may house nests. Discuss flight patterns, smells, feeding, coloring and use of a bird watcher's guide. Try to have several people act as guides who will accompany the children, explain what they are seeing, and answer their questions. Break into small groups for effective observations. Children should be encouraged to record observations, use field glasses, and take pictures. For very young children, producing a language experience chart is a good follow-up to this field trip. Have the students record their observations in some way (a taped account, notes, photographs, or drawings). These records can be used to develop many worthwhile projects—for example, a field guide, photo-journal, games, booklets, mural, etc.

#5 SKILLS:
- Expand writing and research skills.
- Learn about organizations interested in preserving birds and other wildlife.

MATERIALS/RESOURCES:
Each child needs: paper, envelope, stamp (plus 22 cents postage and handling). Write to: American Humane Education Society, 340 South Huntington Avenue, Boston, Mass. 02130 Request: BIRD CARE BOOKLET ("How to care for pet birds," 12 pages).

Each child needs: a postcard and stamp (no additional charges). Write to: Soil Conservation Services, U.S.D.A., P.O. Box 2890, Washington, D.C. 20013. Request: INVITE BIRDS TO YOUR HOME (Specify area of country in which you live.) The book includes pictures and descriptions of birds and of the plants which make good homes and food for birds.

ACTIVITIES:
The children learn to acquire information by writing letters to appropriate sources. Not only does this provide an opportunity to develop letter-writing skills, but also it opens new approaches for research possibilities. Discuss different organizations and government agencies that are concerned with the environment and the preservation of wildlife. If possible, invite a speaker from the Audubon Society, or special government agency to tell the children about their special work and goals.

Have children record information using a means compatible with their level of development:
    notes
    a checklist
    a picture chart
    a tape recorder
Be sure to allow time for discussion and questions. Follow up with a thank-you from the children (simple drawings signed by the children with a cover letter, a thank-you letter, a phone call expressing appreciation.)

#6 SKILLS:
- Read to answer questions and acquire information.
- Develop library, study and research skills.

- Develop positive values and attitudes.
- Expand vocabulary.
- Read from wide variety of books (fact, fantasy, folklore and poetry) for enjoyment.
- Learn to classify and code information.
- Compile information for product development.

RESOURCES / MATERIALS:
Provide access to books, magazines, reference books and other reading materials related to the topic. These materials should cover a wide range of interest and ability levels.

ACTIVITIES:
Gifted primary children need to develop basic library, research and study skills in order to function effectively as independent learners. Habits are being formed to support a lifetime of inquiry; and research. Guide children in these early efforts and help them to select books related to their particular interests. Provide direct instruction in research and study skills and give the children ample opportunity for guided practice.

As children view the beautiful illustrations and photographs usually found in books about birds, they develop aesthetic appreciation. Games can be used to promote vocabulary growth and help children broaden concepts. Materials developed by gifted youngsters often serve as a useful learning resource for their fellow students.

The following is an example of an activity which combines all these factors.

Children can expand vocabulary and develop concepts as they practice basic research skills. Each topic on the learning web is designated by a certain color. Each child selects a topic and prints his/her choice on a color coded index card. Several blank cards of this same color are then given to the youngsters.

As the children come across words related to their topics they do not fully understand, they print each word on a separate index card. The child learns to use a dictionary or other source of information to define the word. Of course, gifted children are often intrigued with words and young lexicographers may choose to include words they comprehend but find so interesting that they want to add them to the collection.

Sample Vocabulary:

FOOD
        nectar
        suet
        vegetarian
        prey
        scavenger

HOMES
        habitat
        territory
        instinct
        burrows
        fibers

PARTS
        preen
        filaplumes
        syrinx
        molting
        down

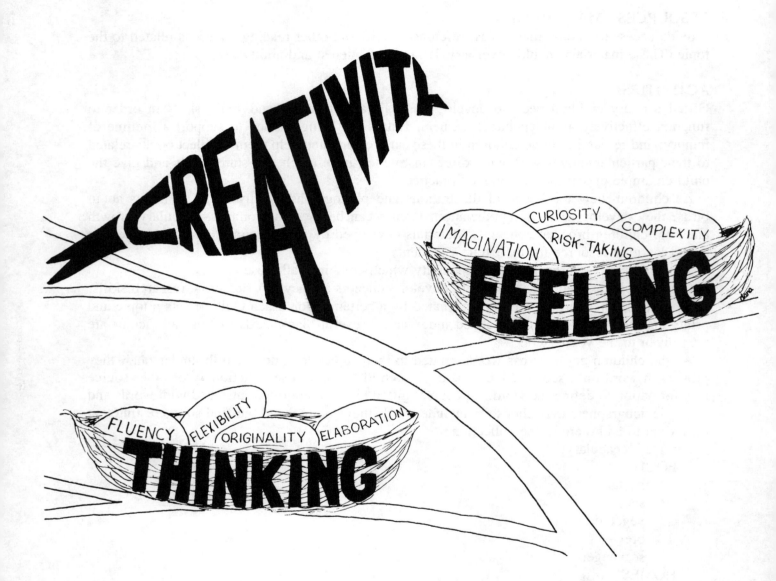

There are many innovative ways these vocabulary cards may be used as a learning resource in the classroom:

1) MINI-DICTIONARY. A dictionary related to a special topic delights the child and provides a simple relevant source of information for classmates. The youngster alphabetizes all his/her word cards and places the topic card on top. Holes may be punched and yarn, ring clasps or other means may be used to secure the cards and form a booklet.

2) THE MATCH GAME. The child uses two color coded cards for each word and writes the same number on the back of each of the two cards. S/he then prints a word on one and the definition on the other. As the numbers increase, so does the pile and packing trays can serve as handy holders. This serves as a simple card game for one or two children. They can see who matches the most cards correctly (or devise other ways of playing). When checking definitions, they simply turn the cards over to see if the numbers match.

3) A MOBILE. A mobile that grows may be constructed by using a branch (or coat hanger) hung in a safe, readily accessible place. Attach a long piece of yarn to each topic card. Secure each topic card firmly to the branch. As the children define and record new words, they simply fasten the vocabulary card to the yarn dangling from their particular topic.

These introductory-level activities are not only enjoyable, but they are also thought igniters.

Creativity

Task cards encourage children to engage in divergent thinking and develop independence as they reinforce and expand their language arts skills. Be sure to have all art supplies and other resources and materials the card may suggest readily available. If a card encourages a child to tell a story, plan to set aside a block of time for sharing this and other such activities.

The following ideas may suggest creative and innovative ways to develop task cards for primary children.

FLUENT THINKING—How many ways do birds help us? (Tell; make a list or chart; draw a picture or mural.)

FLEXIBLE THINKING—Can you rearrange the letters in these scrambled words to make the names of some birds you know? (What else can you do with the words? Make a puzzle or riddle; form a design.)

ORIGINAL THINKING—The little bird looked into my window and . . . [please finish]. (Tell or write a story; plan a puppet show.)

COMPLEXITY—Make a new bird from parts of other birds. (Use cut-up coloring books or magazine pictures; design your own; use art materials. Name your bird.)

RISK TAKING—How would you help a bird who fell from its nest? (Plan a skit or role play. Include the mother bird's reaction.)

ELABORATION—Give this bird some feathers. (Use paints, string art, pine cones, or other art media. Design a home for your bird.)

IMAGINATION—What would happen if you climbed into a big bird's nest? (Plan a skit or pantomime; write a story.)

CURIOSITY—How do birds learn to fly? How do they learn to make their nest? Where can you learn about birds? (Use books, magazines, and other resources to plan a research project.)

Moral Development

According to Piaget, children progress through sequential stages of moral development. Morality for young children is incorporated into their character and displayed in their behavior. Primary children learn to perceive and understand values through experiences.

The teacher guides moral development when the classroom climate encourages children to develop positive attitudes, such as courtesy, conservation, cooperation, tolerance, and concern for others. Children need to practice skills of moral reasoning and acquire positive behavioral traits, including honesty, responsibility, and insight.

Young gifted children are often sensitive and concerned with attitudes, feelings, and values. They do not comprehend values in the abstract but learn from what they see, feel, and experience as they work and play together.

In order to deal with this important aspect of child development, the basic skills of moral reasoning must be identified as behavioral goals. They can be integrated into the primary program through specific strategies.

The following activities help children become skillful in making value-based choices and holding to those values.

Moral reasoning may be introduced through literature and other reading-related activities. Classics such as Aesops Fables are timeless and well suited to this task. Children practice thinking skills for basic problem solving as they:

identify characters and the problem.

review related story facts.

evaluate cause and effect.

consider possible alternatives.

judge the fable's solution.

Through discussion, some children can integrate the knowledge and understanding of moral precepts gained from the fable. Others may choose to respond in a creative way and act out their impression through dramatic play, various art media, or puppetry.

"The Lion and the Mouse" holds a charmed spot as a favorite with many a primary youngster. The children relate to the tiny mouse and delight in a message that values the contributions of all, no matter how small or insignificant they may appear to be. The youngsters do gain insight and apply this message in many classroom situations. It is not unusual to hear remarks such as:

— "If we all pick up one itty bitty thing the whole mess will disappear."

— "My star makes the tree look much happier."

— "If I didn't put the cups on the tray no one would get juice today."

Certainly the ability to prize even a small contribution helps children develop an improved self-concept and positive attitude. Moreover, as the children listen to or read the fables, they are provided with many opportunities to understand the complexity of human behavior.

Another technique for encouraging children to deal with a wide range of emotions and problems is exposing them to an open-ended story. Such a story may be introduced in a number of ways:

(1) The teacher may simply read a story that presents a problem with which the children can readily identify. As the children discuss the situation and try to come up with a solution, they develop problem-solving skills. They must consider the available information, identify with the characters, and make decisions and judgments.

(2) A picture that suggests a dilemma usually provokes frank comments about the scene portrayed. The children start thinking and come to see the problem by focusing on the facts

Baby bear is crying. It is raining. He cannot go to the picnic. Mother bear says, "Don't cry. We will _____."

Can you write an ending for this story? Draw a picture too.

suggested in the picture. As they verbalize their responses they must clarify their own attitudes, feelings, and values.

(3) An open-ended story card allows children to deal with a wide range of emotions and problems. Youngsters learn to empathize with the feelings and problems of others. These cards may be used for discussion or creative writing.

The following are some questions to accompany the story card included in the text:

— How do you think Baby Bear feels?

— Have you ever been promised something you didn't get? How did you act?

— How does Mother Bear feel?

— What do you think Baby Bear will say to his mother?

As the children cope with Baby Bear's dilemma, they come to appreciate the mother's role and feelings. They realize the value of flexible attitudes and behavior as circumstances alter situations.

There are many possibilities for developing cards that help children understand and cope with their world. The story cards on pets and on zoo animals are examples. Questions on task cards may guide children in developing an appreciation of those values that are basic to our cultural heritage—for example:

— Do animals have rights?

— What about the rights of wild animals, zoo animals, animals used in research, and pets?

— Why do some pet owners have problems with their neighbors?

Remember that children must develop an understanding of and commitment to our cultural values and principles through their own efforts.

Many spinoff activities may be developed as children learn to explore their own attitudes and consider the reactions and opinions of others. Possible experiences may include:

● affirming beliefs through the creation of a poster, mural, puppet show, or pet care booklet.

● exploring divergent viewpoints by carrying out a survey on animals and tabulating the results.

● exploring different views further by contacting concerned individuals and organizations dedicated to animal welfare.

● organizing a pet show to demonstrate pride in ownership.

Many other opportunities exist for developing positive traits and helping children set goals for responsible behavior. Role playing encourages a child to develop an understanding of the feelings and viewpoints of others. The following are some suggestions for role-playing situations which hold meaning for primary students:

1. Your neighbor's cat just had kittens and you'd like to have one. Your mom thinks the idea isn't a good one since the family already has a dog for a pet.

2. You are the keeper of a small zoo which allows children to pet animals. Some children are handling a baby goat too roughly and you talk to them.

Awareness of how others may perceive our actions and empathy for their problems may develop as a result of such role-playing activities.

Gifted children must be provided with ample opportunity to practice skills of moral reasoning and develop decision-making abilities. As they grow to cherish their own values, they must develop a tolerance and respect for the views of others.

Many opportunities for role playing as a way of developing empathy and mutual respect are also presented by day-to-day encounters in the classroom. Moral judgment may be based on rational operations, but this needs to be integrated with affective factors in order to help a child gain insight into and sensitivity for the viewpoints of others. Helping children work through real-life problems by the means of role playing allows them to confront conflicts on different levels of reasoning and awareness and to achieve a broadened perspective.

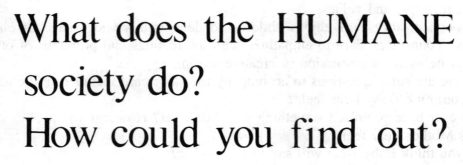

What does the HUMANE society do?
How could you find out?

Pretend you are a
kitten waiting for
a new home.
Tell your story.

Pretend you are the zoo keeper. Make a list of rules for boys and girls. Tell them ways to be kind to the animals.

Did you ever visit a zoo where children can pet and feed the animals?

Young gifted children frequently are socially aware and sensitive to the needs and concerns of others. Through cooperative work and play in the classroom, they acquire concepts of social justice and an understanding of our democratic way of life as well as greater cognitive maturity.

Young children tend to view any act that does not conform to the rules as bad and punishable. The teacher can help youngsters understand that rules of behavior can develop through mutual consent rather than a rigid code. It is important for even very young children to be involved in setting guidelines for classroom and playground behavior. Young children need guidance to build the mutual respect and gain the perspective needed to work out problems related to group living. Quietly talking these things over with the children helps them gain insight into their own intentions and behavior. Role playing can also be used successfully to help children develop the empathy which is essential to building concepts of social justice. They need to realize that their actions also influence their peers for better or worse.

Incidents such as the following one may occur routinely at school. Role playing can provide a viable way of spontaneously resolving them. A teacher witnessed three children standing on the other side of the playground engaged in an angry discussion. One child slapped another across the face, causing the youngster to cry. Of course, slapping is not considered acceptable behavior, and the rules suggested that offenders be sent off to read or play alone. The teacher promptly went to the scene of the "crime." There were two courses of action open: either the teacher could punish the "crime" by sending the offender off to the bench or play the role of a judge and use discretionary power. The teacher chose the latter and found out that the child who had committed the offense had been told by the other two that they didn't want to play with anyone who wore dirty clothes. (The child's clothes were in fact clean but worn.) The teacher discussed the incident with the children and explained that their cruel and exclusionary behavior had made their classmate angry enough to slap one of them. They came to realize that even though slapping was indeed against the rules, they were in some measure responsible for influencing the other child to react by slapping. Who broke the rule? How does it feel to be excluded from a group for whatever reason? What behavior should be considered wrong?

Daily life in the classroom should provide children with the time and opportunity to develop an understanding of the relationship between acts and punishments and to suggest alternate solutions to their problems. They need many opportunities to participate cooperatively in order to reinforce concepts of justice and develop values to live by.

chapter 5

ADAPTING THE LEARNING ENVIRONMENT FOR GIFTED CHILDREN IN THE INTERMEDIATE GRADES

Adapting the Learning Environment for Gifted Children in the Intermediate Grades

Ask yourself, *"Do I measure up as a teacher of gifted children?"* *"Yes, if . . .*

> *I am aware that the special traits, needs, and abilities of gifted children require differentiated learning experiences.*

> *I take advantage of in-service opportunities and keep informed about current trends, research, and publications concerning gifted education.*

> *I explore a wide variety of methods, research, and materials in order to provide challenges in the learning environment.*

> *I realize that it takes effort, planning, and patience to monitor the progress and evaluate the growth of gifted children.*

> *I foster a classroom climate that encourages questioning, responsibility, independence, and creative behavior.*

> *I am tuned in and sensitive to affective needs and offer guidance and support to the children.*

> *I search for opportunities to expand the horizons of gifted children and extend their learning experiences beyond the classroom.*

You should consider yourself a facilitator of gifted children's learning experiences, not an imparter of knowledge.

I am aware that the special traits, needs, and abilities of gifted children require differentiated learning experiences.

Are some types of learning experiences more appropriate for gifted children? Some common trends, methods, and materials used in the education of gifted children are readily discernible in a general way:
- There is increased emphasis on learning materials that encourage divergent thinking.
- More in-depth studies are encouraged rather than generalized overviews of concepts and topics in content areas.

- There is a focus on independent study of special-interest topics.
- Outside experiences are integrated to make classroom experiences more relevant.
- Affective needs, attitudes, feelings, and values are recognized through values clarification programs.
- Simulation and role-playing activities are encouraged.
- There is expanded use of a wide variety of media in order to add variety and dimensionality to studies.
- Open-ended questions are used to foster the development of critical thinking abilities.
- Process-oriented learning activities are stressed rather than a narrow focus on the product.
- Community resources, mentors, and non-traditional approaches to learning are utilized.
- Career awareness and links to the world of work are pursued.

I take advantage of in-service opportunities and keep informed about current trends, research, and publications concerning gifted education.

A qualified teacher is a primary factor in providing a receptive learning environment for the gifted child. How can you make provisions for the gifted children in your classroom? Areas in which the professional in the classroom must function with a high degree of expertise include:

> assessment of needs
>
> planning curricula suitable for the gifted
>
> management skills

A teacher who keeps up to date on journal articles and other reading materials can relate and apply much of this material to classroom procedures. This also provides a basis for the professionally sophisticated teacher to evaluate his/her own attitudes, specific training, and skills in working with gifted students.

An important first step towards professional excellence is gained through self-evaluation of classroom performance. Be prepared to fill in gaps in your professional background and experience. Ask yourself what is necessary to bring your performance up to par. Based on personal choice or your individual needs, schedule, or financial resources, you may wish to become involved in:

> discussion groups
>
> in-service workshops
>
> selected readings
>
> college courses
>
> conferences
>
> program visitations

The important factor is that you improve teaching by actively sharpening your skills, seeking information, and applying it in your classroom on a day-to-day basis. Start slowly, perhaps in one content area. You will grow both in your understanding of the gifted students in your classroom and in your ability to plan appropriate curricula activities for them.

You may also become an agent for change by sharing your insights and innovative ideas with other staff members. Teacher centers offer many exciting opportunities for teachers to plan and share methods, insights, and a variety of data with other skilled classroom practitioners.

I explore a wide variety of methods, resources, and materials in order to provide challenges in the classroom.

In order to meet effectively the needs of all the children within the regular classroom, a teacher must focus on individualized approaches to learning. Content must be modified and teaching methods differentiated when planning for individual differences. The emphasis must change from grade-level texts and materials to multi-level resources and alternate modes of instruction.

Goals and personalized plans must be based on realistic expectations of individual needs. Gifted children must be provided with challenging activities to avoid boredom, laziness, and faulty study habits. These students must be motivated to stretch the limits of their capabilities.

Gifted children vary not only in their abilities but also in their limitations, and they need divergent approaches to learning and to expressing the results of their efforts. Interest and motivation run high when students create original materials by using the many different kinds of audio-visual equipment available.

Learning and communicating effectively with machines is naturally a part of a child's world today. A gifted child's ability to do research, outline, write, and edit material may result in a documentary produced by using an overhead projector and tape recorder. The written report for the teacher to read, mark, and return is no longer the only possible product.

The entire class benefits from innovative audio-visual efforts. The students have an opportunity to work alone as well as in a group effort. They learn to interrelate ideas and value the contributions of others in the class. Thus, the ideas as well as the artistic and technical skills of children of varying ability levels can be called into play in the production process.

Even if you are not comfortable or familiar with various types of machines, computers, and audio-visual equipment, try using them. Read the manuals that accompany such equipment and learn with the children. Ask other staff members for assistance or attend a brief course. Explore and challenge yourself with new and exciting tools for teaching and learning.

Some of the following resources and methods provide exciting opportunities for learning that either augment or take the place of more routine approaches:

> newspapers
> task cards
> learning centers
> learning kits
> trade/professional journals
> community resources
> mentors
> units
> contracts/independent study
> mini-courses

Offering multiple resources and varying the format and pattern of curricular activities allow for learning and intellectual development on many levels.

I realize that it takes effort, planning, and patience to monitor the progress and evaluate the growth of gifted children.

Gifted children often set very high standards for themselves and wonder frequently how they are doing in any given activity. They need the teacher's guidance in setting realistic goals and help in devising a method for monitoring their own progress.

Every effort should be made to avoid pressure and to evaluate the child's growth in a positive, constructive manner. Rather than focus on grades, emphasize personal achievement and help the student value learning for its own sake.

Encourage growth toward independence and responsible behavior by allowing the child to plan, work at, and evaluate tasks. Let the student keep a cumulative folder of work, activities, and tests. Discuss goals and evaluation criteria for the different types of activities in which the student will engage. Gifted children usually grasp factual material quickly and complete skills development exercises with ease. In these areas, differentiated tests may be given on an individual basis or in small groups. These can be mostly self-correcting exercises.

Have each child keep a student planning sheet on a daily or weekly basis, depending on the child's developmental level. This will make it easier for the youngster to structure time, efforts, and materials for any given task.

Evaluation and assessment of each child's progress should be continuous and ongoing. The avenues through which evaluation can take place are:

> student evaluation of his/her progress
> teacher evaluation of student performance
> peer evaluation

It is helpful to have brief teacher-student conferences which include the child's participation in evaluation and activities planning. Frequent, brief conferences provide valuable support for a gifted child's efforts. A child needs to ask questions and wants the teacher's reactions and suggestions on independent projects.

In a program of independent study, gifted children require nurturance and ongoing interaction with the teacher. It is not enough for the teacher to help a student choose a topic, organize a schedule, and point the child in the direction of the library. Indeed, this point only marks the beginning of the process. Sensitive and inquiring students may be reluctant to seek your help if the behavioral expectations are for them to work alone. The children may encounter problems, want to discuss new ideas, and need to re-focus the direction of the study. If teacher involvement is lacking, and each child is simply put on his/her own, the resultant student behavior may be anxiety, loss of motivation, and increased demands for attention in other areas. Students grow in independence when personal efforts are balanced by the dynamics of teacher interaction and support.

Conferences help a student identify specific strengths and weaknesses and offer an opportunity to discuss ways to overcome problems. Help of this nature encourages the child to assume responsibility for skills practice and for his/her own learning, a most significant factor in growth and development. (A sample conference sheet is included in this chapter.)

Children learn from each other. They should be encouraged to work together in pairs or small groups. Effective peer interaction is essential to the learning process. Such sociality provides expanded opportunities for learning from each other, encourages divergent thinking, facilitates the communication of ideas, and fosters problem-solving abilities. They can proofread, edit, and make suggestions about each other's materials. Children learn rather quickly to assess the reasons for their peers' negative and positive reactions to a project. This provides each child with the opportunity to learn to value the opinions of others, even though these may be different from his or her own.

I foster a classroom climate that encourages questioning, responsibility, independence, and creative behavior.

How do you manage your classroom? What type of structure do you employ? Do you involve your students in classroom management? Resourcefulness and leadership skills are developed when students have a voice in planning routines in the classroom. A teacher who encourages students to become involved in management activities gains in flexibility and has more time to guide learning activities. Knowing and understanding the reasons for routines and rules provides children with a feeling of security. An additional bonus is gained in the area of discipline, since all students are encouraged to move in the direction of personal responsibility and accountability for their behavior.

Let's Talk

Name

Time

_____   _____

_____   _____

_____   _____

_____   _____

_____   _____

_____   _____

Please sign up for a conference

The classroom can and should provide daily practice for living in our democracy. Elections can be held, routine jobs can be rotated, and students can be helped to value the needs and contributions of all. Gifted students need the challenge offered by planning procedures to make their learning environment responsive to their concerns. Assignments can be rotated so that routine tasks are shared and challenging jobs are open to those who want to try their hand at them.

Above all, these jobs should not be mere pacifiers handed out by the teacher. Gifted children especially must have meaningful tasks to perform. If the experiences are to promote independence and leadership skills, students must be allowed input into structuring rules, planning activities, and monitoring their own progress. The teacher should serve as a guide and facilitator and be open to their ideas and suggestions. Gifted children flourish in a responsive and open classroom climate that provides practice in responsible sharing of needs on a day-to-day basis.

Solving problems develops skills of critical thinking and has genuine impact when applied to issues in the classroom that are important to the children. Learning by doing applies to problem-solving experiences throughout a gifted child's school career. Teachers should realize that children need to live fully in their present on preparation for the future.

What influences the development of creativity? Many authorities agree that independent thought and freedom of expression should be encouraged. Adult standards should not be imposed and the teacher should encourage children's questions and original products. Creativity flourishes in a classroom where the children are allowed to interact, explore, and manipulate materials whenever they need to express an idea. Children should be encouraged to write, produce, and express their own thoughts and ideas. It is difficult to develop creativity in children when the learning atmosphere tends to be over regimented with heavy emphasis on drill and routine.

Basic skills can be practiced, expanded, and mastered in creative and innovative ways. Emphasis should be on cooperative sharing of the products children create and other ways of demonstrating and communicating information.

I am tuned in and sensitive to affective needs and offer guidance and support to the children.

The basis of all guidance is understanding of the individual. If children are to achieve their potential, they must possess an understanding of themselves and their abilities, interests, and opportunities. Gifted children need a classroom environment sensitive enough to meet their emotional needs. As the classroom teacher, you must help them develop positive self-images. This is conducive to their emotional well-being and essential to their learning and future achievement.

It is important to consider the affective, as well as the cognitive, needs of a child when planning learning activities. A teacher must understand that the child's traits and nature may sometimes have a negative effect on social behavior. Encourage acceptance of him or herself and acceptance of others. Be aware of problems of motivation, adjustment, and peer relationships. The child may feel rejected or isolated and have a need for peer relations in many types of groups.

A child may dislike routine, behave negatively, and resist interruption of his/her special activities. At other times, the child may experience frustration and become excessively self-critical. The sensitivity and awareness of gifted children often causes them to probe and worry about philosophical issues related to global human concerns.

The classroom climate should encourage children to adopt positive values, interact effectively with others, and develop wholesome attitudes toward themselves. There are a number of ways this can be accomplished. First and foremost is the relationship of mutual trust and respect that needs to develop between teacher and student. Other helpful approaches to positive social and emotional development may include:

a values clarification program
informal rap sessions
group discussions
debates
personal journals
reading literature
role playing and simulation games
drama or puppetry
poetry or creative writing
producing a student newspaper
interviews, questionnaires, and opinion polls

This list is by no means inclusive and merely serves as an indicator of the types of activities that are useful.

I search for opportunities to expand the gifted child's horizons and opportunities for learning beyond the classroom.

A comprehensive program of education for the gifted child extends enrichment beyond the confines of your classroom. It intricately weaves a web of knowledgeable people, interesting places, and stimulating resources and materials not ordinarily available to the students. Exposure to new ideas breathes life into your program and provides ingredients for first-hand learning experiences.

Communications skills are sharpened and children are provided with role models when they meet professionals, skilled artisans and other community members. They can explore and discover special interests and gain insight into potential careers or vocations.

Be prepared for the unexpected when dealing with gifted children who are divergent and creative thinkers. A trip to the museum is usually designed to provide extended resource information related to a particular unit or theme. This may indeed inspire many gifted and average students to reconstruct a miniature Egyptian Temple to scale and engage in other related enrichment activities. However, gifted children may not wish to pursue suggested follow up activities but prefer to follow newly opened avenues of personal interest: Who found and reconstructed the articles? How are they preserved? Who vouches for their authenticity? Who selects which articles are to be displayed? A teacher must assist such children in developing research skills on a more personalized basis (e.g., writing a letter to the curator of the museum, arranging a visit with a professor of archaeology, helping parents plan a behind-the-scenes visit to the museum facilities).

The quest for knowledge by an eager, probing young mind challenges a teacher to provide ever spiraling links to a wider and wider range of human and material resources. Moreover, experiences such as field trips, work with mentors, museum visits, nature hikes, mini courses, and the like add to children's understanding of themselves and the world around them.

When a child shows a particular aptitude or special talent, a classroom teacher should seek the support of resource people, such as teachers of art, music, reading or any other specialty. These curriculum specialists can help you to plan appropriate learning activities. They may be able to schedule some additional time to work with the child or suggest talented older students or community members who may serve as a mentor. Parents may wish to augment the school program by providing their talented children with lessons or additional learning and enrichment experiences. Discuss your observations with them and offer encouragement and any available information.

It takes initiative, effort and planning on your part to arrange out-of-class learning experiences.

Perhaps other staff members may want to work with you in a cooperative effort that will benefit not only the youngsters but also increase community support for the school and its programs.

How Can the Classroom Teacher Adapt Instruction for the Gifted Child?

1. According to his/her developmental level, involve the child in planning, working at, and evaluating tasks.

2. Encourage personal growth and self-realization through the development of positive values and attitudes.

3. Use teaching/learning strategies which emphasize higher-level thinking abilities.

4. Provide tasks that include open-ended learning activities, small group work, and discussion.

5. Develop learning-process skills that enhance problem-finding and solving abilities through independent projects.

6. Maintain a learning environment that provides opportunity, materials, and a climate suitable for developing creativity.

7. Utilize materials, media, and resources in order to stimulate in-depth learning.

Remember a gifted child needs qualitatively different learning experiences, not just more of the same.

Language Arts:
The Thread of Learning

A receptive environment for a gifted child stems from the regular school program. Enrichment both encompasses and extends basic learning experiences in various curriculum areas.

The language arts may be considered the integrating factor or heart of the elementary program. Perceiving, reading writing, speaking and listening form a communications core to support the gifted child's cognitive and affective development. The child understands, develops and clarifies his/her values through communication processes. Language provides the foundation for social experiences and life skills as well as academic goals.

These processes entail learning specific skills and procedures. These skills cannot be taught in isolation, but can be fused with the content areas through the language arts. Children's language experiences should be meaningful to them. The students must have genuine interest in the activities if they are actually going to share ideas and develop higher-level thought processes.

In content areas, it's not just reading the assignment, but rather reading to answer questions and solve problems out of curiosity and interest. Pursuing an individual goal through independent activities adds spice and motivation to learning. In this way there is a real need for critical thinking at different levels of awareness.

The keys to independent learning are found in the mastery and expansion of these language arts skills. Assessing child's skills development is important and the teacher needs to monitor growth and evaluate progress.

Gifted children are often clever verbally. Help them develop basic understandings and guard against glib generalizations that may mask a lack of fundamental facts.

After diagnosing the students' strengths and weaknesses, ample opportunity must be provided in daily activities to expand basic language skills. The following: INDIVIDUAL PROGRESS RECORD LANGUAGE ARTS - SKILLS DEVELOPMENT (Listening, Speaking, Reading, Writing) and INDIVIDUAL SUMMARY SHEET, LANGUAGE ARTS SKILLS DEVELOPMENT are helpful for planning differentiated activities and in evaluating the child's progress. The skills listed indicate some of the processes in which a child needs to become involved. Plan for developing communication skills on a personalized basis for a particular child. Work with that child to set a few simple goals that:

- Deal with skills that are readily attainable by the child at this stage of his/her development.
- Motivate and are related to some current interest and effort of the child.

Take into account a child's personality and behavior traits as well as academic needs. There are numerous ways a child can develop the same cluster of skills.

Be sure to set up a section in your classroom such as an "Author's Workshop" with a wide variety of appropriately advanced reference books and other challenging resources and materials. This encourages the independent pursuit of language skills by the gifted child.

ENRICHMENT PROGRAM - INDIVIDUAL PROGRESS RECORD

LANGUAGE ARTS - SKILLS DEVELOPMENT - LISTENING

Student _____

Skills	Goals	Methods-Materials	Progress-Evaluation
Listens with sustained involvement.			
Evaluates and interprets messages.			
Reacts to humor			
Retains and applies information.			
Follows complicated oral directions.			
Listens to radio, records and tapes for information and enjoyment.			
Listens for a specific purpose.			
Aware of speaker's tone and inflection, perceiving attitudes other than explicitly spoken message.			
Understands irony, sarcasm, exaggeration.			
Judicial use of aides such as a tape recorder that support reflective listening and analysis of important data.			
Aware and sensitive to environmental sounds.			
Appreciates and tries to understand differences in dialect.			
Listens for enjoyment and enrichment--stories, poetry, drama			

LANGUAGE ARTS - SKILLS DEVELOPMENT - SPEAKING

Student _____

Skills	Goals	Methods-Materials	Progress-Evaluation
Advanced, accurate vocabulary usage.			
Gives directions skillfully.			
Expresses self with wit, humor.			
Oral fluency, talks with ease.			
Clear, expressive and precise oral communication.			
Articulates own questions and needs.			
Interviews, introduces visitors and community mentors.			
Uses courtesy phrases and titles where appropriate.			
Uses the phone to acquire information, schedule trips.			
Familiar with Parliamentary Procedure.			
Expresses tolerance for viewpoint of others.			
Participates in group inquiry, discussion, oral reports.			
Understands and sticks to a topic.			
Participates in drama, choral speaking.			
Refined, clear oral reading techniques.			
Expressive voice quality and tone.			
Recites poetry with proper rhythm and inflection.			

ENRICHMENT PROGRAM - INDIVIDUAL PROGRESS RECORD

Student _____

LANGUAGE ARTS - SKILLS DEVELOPMENT - READING

Skills	Goals	Methods-Materials	Progress-Evaluation
Exceptional mastery of vocabulary.			
Aware of different shades of meaning in similar words.			
Enjoys using vocabulary for the fun and challenge crossword puzzles provide.			
Comprehends and infers meaning of material read.			
Aware of cultural values and heritage through literature.			
Studies origin and derivation of words.			
Extensive reading in a variety of areas.			
Interrelates ideas.			
Mastery of study skills.			
Understands multiple-step directions.			
Adjusts rate of reading to suit purpose.			
Understands maps, legends, diagrams.			
Can predict and verify outcomes.			
Reads to find answers to questions.			
Distinguishes fact and opinion.			
Uses reference materials efficiently.			
Can read critically and evaluate information.			
Understands technical vocabulary, content areas.			

ENRICHMENT PROGRAM - INDIVIDUAL PROGRESS RECORD

Student _____

LANGUAGE ARTS - SKILLS DEVELOPMENT - WRITING

Skills	Goals	Methods-Materials	Progress-Evaluation
Advanced mastery and use of vocabulary.			
Proficient in form, technique and structure of written language.			
Interrelates oral and written language.			
Good typist, legible handwriting.			
Can summarize and outline.			
Assembles and edits materials.			
Takes notes, records information.			
Prepares written reports.			
Writes to acquire information.			
Refined mechanics in various forms of letter writing.			
Writes news stories and editorials.			
Writes directions for games, etc.			
Organizes lists for jobs, materials, etc.			
Writes biographies and auto-biographies.			
Can critique plays, concerts, movies.			
Can develop information charts and folios.			
Prolific expression of own thoughts and ideas in a variety of forms-- stories, poetry, drama.			
Writes creatively.			
Writes with style, persuasion, impact.			
Accurate spelling.			

ENRICHMENT PROGRAM – INDIVIDUAL SUMMARY SHEET

LANGUAGE ARTS – SKILLS DEVELOPMENT

Student _____

goals   progress notes

Reading:

Writing:

Speaking:

Listening:

Research Study Skills _____

Content Area Skills _____

Attitudes and Behavior _____

Special Interests _____

Signed _____
         (teacher)

Date _____

Creativity

Although creativity cannot be taught, classroom conditions can allow it to flourish in children. Not all gifted children are creative, but the teacher can do much to encourage the development of creative behavior by employing certain methods and strategies such as:

brainstorming

problem-solving activities

open-ended questions

focusing on divergent/productive thinking

The components of creative thinking cannot be taught or practiced in isolation. Activities which present the elements that elicit creative responses should be incorporated within the teaching unit. Teachers can encourage children to develop traits of spontaneity and resourcefulness by encouraging independent work and original products. A warm and accepting classroom atmosphere supports intuitive and expressive capabilities.

Some elements of creativity explored by Osborne are outlined on the following page.

Creative Behaviors

Cognitive - Thinking

Fluency - (quantity)

generation of a number of relevant responses

Flexibility - (categories)

variety of classes, ideas and approaches

Originality - (new)

novel uses, unique solutions, clever, subtle, unusual responses

Elaboration - (elaborate, add on to)

give details, expand basic concept, idea

Affective - Feeling

Risk Taking - (courage)

tolerance for ambiguity, take a chance, present, defend ideas

Complexity - (challenge)

pursue difficult tasks, seek alternative actions, organize

Curiosity - (inquisitive)

pursue, discover, explore, reflective thinking, follow up on hunches

Imagination - (intuition)

daydream, fantasize, feel intuitively, pretend, wonder

Developing Higher Level Thinking Skills

It's helpful for teachers to have an understanding of the hierarchy of thinking skills based on THE TAXONOMY OF EDUCATIONAL OBJECTIVES: COGNITIVE DOMAIN by Benjamin S. Bloom. Most educators believe that greater instructional emphasis should be placed on developing higher level thinking skills for bright and able youngsters.

Teachers must remember that children need to develop a base of information and be able to relate facts. Lessons should provide practice in the use of facts as tools in understanding and exercising these higher levels of cognition. Youngsters must have basic information before they can grapple with complexities and can solve problems. Replies to data based questions provide a springboard for learning to respond to evaluative questions. Gifted children need to develop their ability in using the inquiry process through many experiences, if they are to find and solve problems.

The accompanying chart is based on Bloom's Taxonomy and will prove helpful when planning lessons and activities. Also particularly helpful is *GEMINI: Gifted Education Manual for Individualizing Networks of Instruction* by Dr. C. L. Lewis et al.

A Chart Based on

Bloom's Taxonomy of the Cognitive Domain

Different Levels of Thinking

Classification	Question Cues	Student Activity
6 Evaluation	(judging) Can you set standards, rate, select and choose, decide, weigh according to, how do you feel about	Criticize, justify choices and actions, decide according to standard, prove
5 Synthesis	(creating, adapting) Think of all the different ways, how else, can you design, improve, develop	Imagine, predict, design, improve, change, create, invent, adapt
4 Analysis	(seeing parts of) How can you, What are causes, consequences, steps of process, can you arrange, examine	Compare, take apart, analyze, solve, contrast, dissect, investigate, discuss
3 Application	(using, solving problems) Can you use the information, demonstrate, can you solve	Apply, model, order, use acquired data in new learning situations, operate
2 Comprehension	(showing that you understand) Can you tell in your own words, interpret, explain, what are the relationships	Classify, demonstrate, group, illustrate, rearrange, reorder
1 Knowledge	(finding out) Can you tell, list, describe, do you remember, relate, who, when, where, which, what, define	Memorize, data gathering, name, observe, show, record, locate

Abstract

Concrete

The classroom teacher can help the gifted child gather data and process information by planning questions and learning experiences utilizing the different thinking levels.

Developing Differentiated Learning Experiences

There are two main areas of concern for the classroom teacher in meeting the needs of a gifted child:

1) Assessing individual needs and preparing an individual program plan
2) Providing differentiated learning experiences based on unique traits, needs and abilities of the gifted child. The teacher needs to deal with effective ways to provide differentiated learning experiences in both the cognitive and affective areas. Plan for individual needs by considering these factors:

   level of maturity

   prior experiences

   interests, abilities and behavioral traits

   preferred learning modality

   level of skills development

Differentiated learning occurs when the following conditions are tailored to meet these needs on a personalized basis.

- degree of student involvement in planning and evaluation
- content, structure and format of learning experiences
- level and type of resources and materials
- affective needs, support services and guidance
- out of class experiences

Start small. Select a content area and review a particular unit or lesson plan you have used successfully, considering these points:

- How are the levels of cognitive complexity utilized in activities? (Use Bloom's Taxonomy as a guide.)
- How could materials, resources and experiences be made more challenging for the gifted child?
- In what ways can the child be involved in planning and evaluating tasks?
- How can questions be structured to promote creativity, problem solving and critical thinking abilities?
- What additional opportunities could be provided for independent study on special interest topics?
- How can opportunities for learning be extended beyond the classroom?
- To what extent can activities be developed that encourage children to apply skills and interrelate ideas?
- Do the learning experiences enable the child to interact positively with others?
- Will the child gain in self-concept and be more able to cope in an independent manner as a result of these learning experiences?
- Do the activities encourage the child to develop and act upon his/her own positive values and beliefs?

The LESSON PLANNING SHEET can serve as a guide as you review and adapt existing lessons for use with the gifted child.

_____

_____

_____

_____

_____

_____

_____

Skill Objectives: _____

_____

_____

_____

Values and Attitudes: _____

_____

_____

Process	Activities	Materials

Evaluation_____

_____

_____

TIME MACHINE — THE PAST

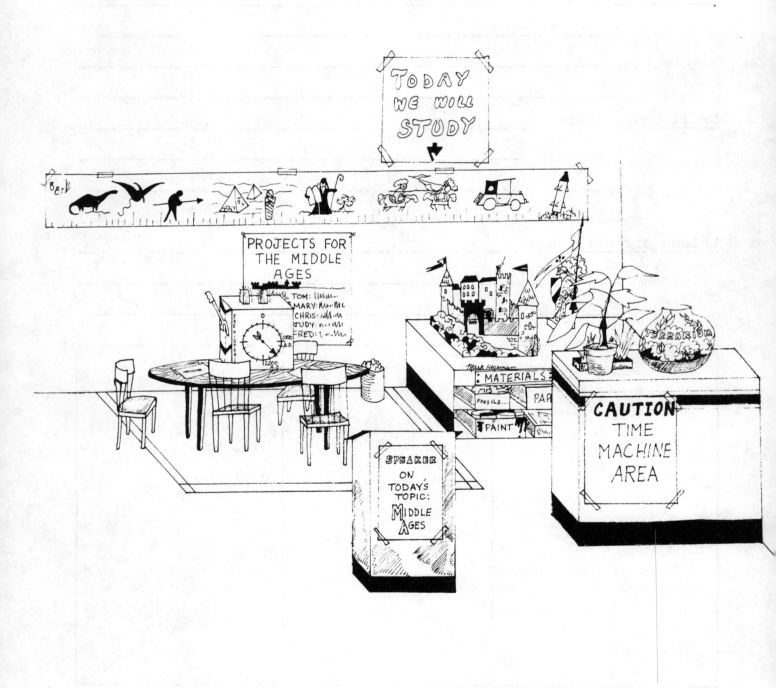

The Learning Center Format

In the intermediate grades lessons for the gifted student must provide challenge and motivation. A gifted youngster often far surpasses peers in the ability to do research and function as an avid independent learner. Advanced communication skills enable a student to accept new challenges and explore new vistas. The teacher responds by differentiating instruction, materials and resources.

As do most children of this age group, gifted children share a sense of adventure. They are intrigued by mystery and exploration. Activities should be presented in a manner that appeals to the students and captures their curiosity.

An example of an innovative lesson is demonstrated by this introduction to a unit dealing with the concept of a time line. The learning center format effectively provides a structural framework for these unit activities on various interest and ability levels. Students develop an understanding of the need for selective research and classifying, recording and using specific facts. This data base is necessary if the youngsters are to deal with problems, explore issues and justify answers in any given time period.

The following question cues are intended to elicit creative student responses and may readily be adapted for use as task cards.

Creativity - Task Cards
Time Machine - The Past or the Future?
  Pick a time which you will visit.

FLUENCY - What things will you see when you land? Tape an account of your arrival.

FLEXIBILITY - Pick one object which you brought with you. List all the ways it might be useful to you.

ORIGINALITY - Who would you like to be in this time? Prepare a brief skit demonstrating both the personality and character of your choice.

ELABORATION - Make up a story to explain to inhabitants how you arrived and why you do or don't "fit in."

RISK TAKING - What would you do and think about if you couldn't get back to the present? Prepare an entry for your journal or diary.

COMPLEXITY - How would each member of your family deal with the problems of the time you landed in? List a few problems. Jot down what you think possible reactions might be. Ask your family to react to the problem situations. Record their answers. How do they compare?

CURIOSITY - If you could stay in that time for a day, a week, or a month, how would you go about gathering data? Outline your plans.

IMAGINATION - If someone from that time landed in the present, how would the present seem to him/her? Conduct a T.V. interview with the time traveler.

TIME MACHINE - THE FUTURE

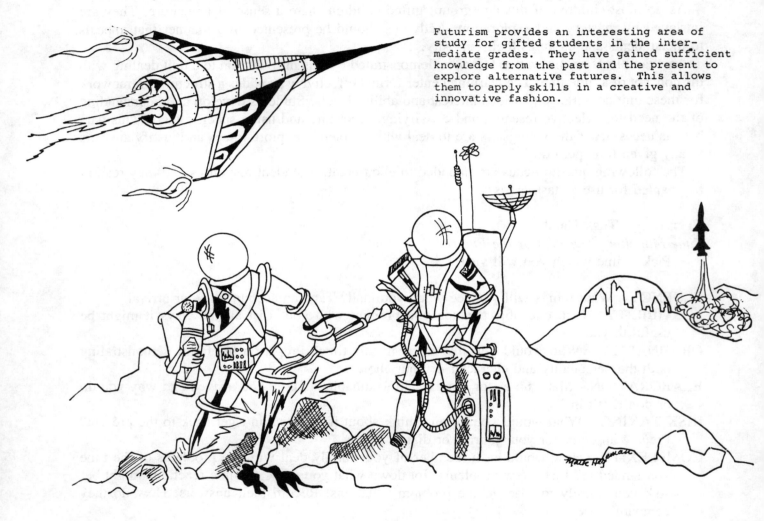

Futurism provides an interesting area of study for gifted students in the intermediate grades. They have gained sufficient knowledge from the past and the present to explore alternative futures. This allows them to apply skills in a creative and innovative fashion.

Travel · Terminal

Where are You?

Where is Peru?

Focus on: PERU

How Would You Travel To: Peru?

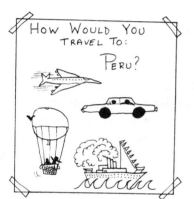

THINGS TO DO:
1. Climb the Andes.
2. Build a City.
3. Make Pottery.
4. Do a Word Find.
5. Be a Travel Agent.
6. Be Curator of a Museum.

TASK ~ CARDS

machu pichu

A   B   C

RESEARCH

TRAVEL MARKER

Travel ... Brochures

PLASTER OF PARIS

DOLLS OF OTHER LANDS

Preparing a Resource Unit

Gifted children respond to teaching methods that integrate areas of knowledge with creative approaches to problem solving. Resource units can be developed that provide open ended learning activities that expand concepts, understandings and values by the following:

1. Involve children in planning unit activities by listing their questions about the unit and developing a flow chart with related activities.
2. Structure activities to meet a wide range of abilities, needs and interests.
3. Provide access to facts, information and resources in order to expand concepts and broaden knowledge.
4. Promote skills development by providing opportunities for responsible independent learning.
5. Encourage the development of desirable behavioral traits and positive work habits.
6. Help children learn how to refocus direction, solve conflicts and evaluate results.

The following Resource Unit on Peru incorporates these principles in various ways.

Resource Unit - Grades 5-6
CONCEPT: CULTURE IN THE MIDDLE ANDES - EMPHASIS ON PERU

GENERAL IDEA:

— Children study the geographical differences that are the origin for separate cultures that co-exist in the lands of the middle Andes. They can relate the past to the present cultures. Thus, they gain insight into the fact that culture is not the monopoly of any one group. They develop an appreciation for work and its contribution to society.

KNOWLEDGE OBJECTIVES:

— The geographic features of the lands of the Andes affect the lives of its inhabitants. •
— Altitude and climate have a direct impact on the culture that develops and on how people live.
— Communities develop different modes of adaptation to different environments.
— Many occupations contribute to economic growth and social welfare.
— The location of key sites is based on their role in meeting the needs of the region and are influenced by many geographic factors.
— The economy and culture of a region is related to land, climate, and natural resources.
— Each country has common economic problems and unique economic problems.
— There are inequities in economic relationships.
— In Peru the physical barriers of altitude and climate are reflected in the inability of the people to unite and form one country and one people.
— Tourism promotes cultural exchange and contributes to the economy.
— The Incas were a highly skilled people.
— Their artistic contributions are still evident in today's art.
— A study of the earlier art can give us a better understanding of past culture and its meanings.
— Agricultural methods of the past still have an application in the present day.
— The methods may have been updated technologically, but the basic concepts remain the same—i.e., irrigation, farming on mountain terraces.

SKILL OBJECTIVES:

— Given facts and evidence on the past and present cultures, the students will be able to make generalizations about the similarities and differences.
— The students will be able to gather resources and prepare materials and plan and arrange an attractive display.
— The students learn to relate and apply concepts.
— Given maps, the students reinforce and expand their skill in map reading.
— The students work and share information in groups.
— Students develop the ability to analyze, compare, discuss concepts.
— The students learn to focus on concepts and prepare creative summary such as travel folder and museum guide.
— Provided with meaningful situations the student makes practical application of knowledge gained about various occupations.
— Given facts about the Peruvian economy and monetary system, a student will be able to apply math skills and compute rate of exchange.
— Students will grow in research skills by actively seeking new sources and avenues of information.
— Promote an attitude of interest, cooperation and concern for peoples of other nations by valuing tourism, student exchange and other areas of communications among peoples.
— Children form an understanding of the many reasons people travel to another country and comprehend cultural differences.

VALUES AND ATTITUDES:

— Students make cross cultural comparisons and gain in knowledge and respect of the rich cultural heritage of Peru.
— They grow in awareness of the economic and social needs of those who struggle in underdeveloped nations.
— They develop an appreciation and respect for the contributions of various occupations to the social and economic welfare of a people.

EVALUATION:

— The teacher's evaluations based on observations and estimate of concepts learned and skills reinforced and expanded have to be individual.
— Informal tests may be developed—matching, multiple choice, completion or essay tests, or locating places on individual outline maps.
— Students should demonstrate evidence of cooperation, courtesy and respect for the ideas and products of their peers.

These activities present the facts and information needed to form a data base which will enable students to engage in higher level thinking skills. (See following page.)

WHERE MAN LIVES INFLUENCES THE WAY HE LIVES.

The geographic features of the lands of the middle Andes affect the lives of the inhabitants.
1. Topography and Physical Features
2. Altitude and Climate
3. Adaptation to Environment

1. TOPOGRAPHY AND PHYSICAL FEATURES

CUE	UNIT ACTIVITIES	MATERIAL
Relief map of South America	Introduction: Explain mapping and map reading analysis as basic tools of geography. How does this map differ from other maps we have studied? Help the students locate the Andes, coastal lowlands, Peru, Bolivia, rivers, etc., on the relief map that is displayed.	*Map may be obtained from the Pan American Union Wash., D.C. 20006*
Show filmstrips on map skills	Reinforce map-reading skills and introduce new areas by showing filmstrips dealing with physical maps and how to study an area through maps.	*Learning to use maps. Reading physical maps. Studying an area through maps. Encyclopedia Britannica.*
Group discussion	Use questions to help students interpret the map and open group discussion: Do the Andes mountains create problems? How do the Andes affect communication and transportation? Why do you think Lima became a major city? How would you travel from New York to Peru? Why? Why were roads so important to the Incas? Are they important today? How would you travel from Lima to Cuzco? Why do you think Peru remains a nation of distinct cultures and people?	
Individual projects	Encourage children to make their own relief map with clay, or manila paper drawing in the different topographical features. The use of creative media reinforces the child's understanding of his newly acquired skill in understanding an area through maps.	*Provide list of features for children to highlight. Shoe box lid, clay, poster paints, 8x10 manila paper, magic markers.*

2. ALTITUDE AND CLIMATE

CUE	UNIT ACTIVITIES	MATERIAL
Resource reading	Make available various books and pamphlets covering the important features of altitude and climate in Peru. Given a specified period of time, the children select and read material and make notes on what they consider salient features.	*Masters, R.V. Peru in Pictures Sterling Pub. Co. Inc. 1972*

CUE	UNIT ACTIVITIES	MATERIAL
Visual aids-pictures	Display pictures which clearly show the three principal regions the Andes mountains divide Peru into: the high plateaus of the mountains, the eastern mountain slopes, and the dry coastal plain. This should reinforce facts gained by independent reading.	*Pictures: Creative Educational Soc., Inc., Mankato, MN.S.A. Peru, Teaching Picture Units.*
Class discussion	Teacher comments on the pictures and asks a few leading questions in order to elicit response and motivate the group. If you were a photo journalist seeking to photograph jungle animals, what part of Peru would you visit? Why is there only one runway at the airport in Lima? Why does Peru export so much fishmeal? Why would a tourist from Lima be likely to experience headaches, dizziness, and so on when visiting the city of Cuzco? What effect does the Humboldt current have on Lima? The trade winds? What would you pack in your suitcase for a trip to Iquitos? To Coata? If you planned to live in Lima for a while, what language would you study?	*Arrange chairs in a semi-circle to facilitate group discussion.*
Read to develop understanding of a different way of life	Through discussion, students explore values and attitudes. The students will grow in awareness and concern for the needs of the people in underdeveloped nations. Students may develop a role-playing situation to examine the inequality of economic oppression.	*Mangurian, D.: Children of the Incas. Four Winds Press, NY, 1979*

3. ADAPTATION TO ENVIRONMENT

CUE	UNIT ACTIVITIES	MATERIAL
Filmstrip on Peru	Reinforces concepts learned by students through readings and group discussions. Introduces an overall view of life-styles and how the people have adapted to the different geographical areas. Explores concept of shelter, agriculture, and transportation in relation to climate and altitude. Provide an opportunity for students to explore the rich cultural heritage of the Incas, Chimus, and other Pre-Inca people. Students will more readily appreciate and understand how their civilization and lifestyle permeates and affects Peru today.	*Filmstrip available from United Nations Film & Visual Information Div., New York*
Class discussion	Students form small groups in an attempt to analyze, compare and discuss concepts of geographical influences on lifestyles in Peru. Relate past and present adaptions to the environment. Teacher provides index cards to group leader with questions to motivate students and facilitate discussion. What similarities can you note between the ruins of Ancon and ancient Egypt? Why is the llama important today as well as in the past? What are the reasons that Cuzco was a metropolis in Inca days and is one today? What climatic factors aided in the development of Peru's city of Lima? Why do you think Pachacamac is no longer a flourishing city? Leaders summarize discussions for class.	

CUE	UNIT ACTIVITIES	MATERIAL
Group Research and projects	Students may work in small groups to collect information. The students may write to Pan American Union, Washington, D.C. 20006 for pamphlets on the agricultural products and systems used in Peru today. They may also write to the United Nations for information. Using the encyclopedias and any other reference materials in the library to gather this information will prove helpful.	*Paper, envelopes & stamps. Reference materials*
View "Legacy of the Incas"—six sound filmstrips: "Who Were the Incas" "Francisco Pizarro" "Conquest of the Incas" "Agriculture" "Engineering & Architecture" "Language, Art & Government" from Educational Enrichment Materials Co. (A company of the New York Times)	These filmstrips provide a wealth of knowledge that helps students gain historical background which is so necessary to understand contemporary Peru. After viewing the filmstrips, students may wish to pursue a special interest in depth through guided independent study.	*Teachers should discuss the filmstrips with the students & ask probing questions that encourage further thought & research, e.g., what sophisticated skills used by the Incas in engineering invite comparison with those used by the Egyptians in building the pyramids or with those which form the basis of our advanced technology. These questions also help a youngster narrow the scope of his/her project & focus on a particular area of study.*

Learning Activities structured according to *Bloom's Taxonomy*

Focus: GEOGRAPHY

SKILLS	KNOWLEDGE
map skills	Use maps, books, etc. What are the physical features and topography of Peru?
research skills	Pretend you are a *pilot* and make a tape describing what you see as you fly over
reading	the country.
interpretation	SPINOFF:
	Pretend you are one of the conquistadors journeying into Peru in 1532. How might you describe the physical features and topography? Compare your description with the pilot's. How are the reports affected by methods of observations, prior information, and historical frame of reference?

SKILLS	COMPREHENSION
writing	How does the topography influence communication among Peru's people? Be a
organizing	government worker whose job is *census taker*. How do the Andes affect
outlining	communication and transportation? Plan your monthly report to your
expanded	supervisor explaining why you are late.
map skills	SPINOFF:
(symbols)	How did the Incan Empire handle communication and transportation? Make a chart demonstrating the methods used. What factors are different today? What remains the same?

SKILLS	APPLICATION
oral language	Be a *tour guide*. Plan and discuss a series of trips for tourists to explore the
organization	regions. Describe the highlights of the itinerary in each of the three regions.
planning	Prepare a travel brochure for each of the regions.
expanded map skills	SPINOFF:
(using a road map)	Prepare a list of helpful hints for the tourists. Discuss:

clothing
transportation
food and water
budgets
health concerns

SKILLS	ANALYSIS
writing	How does the topography affect the way of life for citizens. Plan a *photo*
creative media use	*journalists report*. (Travel folders will provide materials and resources.) Can
research	you think of additional sources?
design	SPINOFF:
plan	Prepare an article for *The New York Times Magazine* section demonstrating
arrange	agricultural methods of the past that still have an application in the present day.
layout	

SKILLS	SYNTHESIS
sensory learning	Pretend you are the *curator of a museum* in the United States. Combine artifacts
[touch, smell,	from the three regions. Assemble your exhibit. Prepare a guide booklet which
feel, etc.]	accurately describes and highlights important facts about the display.

Oral language
Writing
Multi-Media
Art Appreciation
Research
Creative Summary
Problem Solving
Cooperative group
work habits

SPINOFF:
Tape a precise and detailed description of the display so that a blind person can appreciate the artifacts. How does this differ from the guide booklet? What part do the senses play in creating images?

SKILLS:
research skills
Uncovering Sources
of information
Judging according
to criteria
Basic Economics
Use of financial
information
Critical Thinking

EVALUATION:
You are a *business person*. Where will you set up your business and why? Develop criteria and give reasons why you chose one region over the others for your import-export business dealing with handicrafts and ponchos

SPINOFF:
What restrictions might the Peruvian government set on your business?
       financial investment
       capital
       taxes
       profits
How could you find out? How might this affect your decision to locate in an area? Suppose you were a botanist or an archeologist. What restrictions might be placed on your work?

Math for the Gifted Child

When planning for a gifted child's math program, it is important for the classroom teacher to consider the following three points:

1. APPLIED MATHEMATICS holds a special challenge for gifted youngsters. It allows them to see the usefulness of math in many interrelated fields of endeavor. Rather than focus unnecessarily on drill and repetition, able students become adept at applying and expanding math skills. Provide ample opportunity to use scales, rulers, computers, graphs, and other mathematical tools.

2. ENRICHMENT MATHEMATICS develops logical thinking, accuracy, analysis, and habits of inquiry through puzzles and games of logic, strategy, and the like.

3. RAPID PROGRESS MATHEMATICS allows for vertical movement through the math curriculum by gifted children who are endowed with exceptional mathematical ability. Advancement and sequential growth can be accomplished in many ways, such as work with a mentor/tutor (e.g., an older student), use of programmed materials, and an individualized math program. Some of these points are demonstrated below.

INTERRELATING CONTENT AREAS USING BLOOM'S TAXONOMY

Focus: MATHEMATICS — MONEY

KNOWLEDGE: Engage in research using tour books, banks, phone calls to travel agents, etc. to find out the currency used in Peru. (Record sources of information and list monetary facts.)

COMPREHENSION: Make a money exchange board which could be placed in an airport, bank, etc.

APPLICATION: Exchange dollars for soles for "tourists."

ANALYSIS: Is money the only method of exchange? What types of economic classes are in Peru? How did the social structure come about?

SYNTHESIS: Pay for a hotel bill with soles. What is the policy on tipping? (How could you find out?)

EVALUATION: Are workers in Peru receiving a fair wage for their work hours? Compare the standard of living in Peru with that in the United States. (Design a graph that justifies your decision.)

A systematic math series devoted to problem solving strategies is now available for gifted students in the intermediate grades; it is called *Problemoids* and is available from Trillium Press.

Creativity-Task Cards

Focus: OCCUPATIONS

FLUENCY: You are a sociologist who has been asked to prepare a report on the problems of the rural mountain population. List all the problems you think a poor farmer might have in Peru.

FLEXIBILITY: You are an information and public relations official from the Department of Agriculture in Peru. Prepare a news release for foreign agricultural experts telling them how many ways they can use bagasse.

ORIGINALITY: You are an entrepreneur opening a restaurant in Lima that highlights native Peruvian dishes. Prepare a menu (list the dishes). Name your restaurant.

ELABORATION: You are a crafts person. Decorate a gourd as Indians of the Peruvian highlands do.

RISK-TAKING: You have been invited by a farm family in Peru to be an exchange student for a year. Write them a letter accepting or rejecting their offer. In your letter, please explain fully the reasons for your decision. (Discuss the offer with parents, teachers, friends, and any exchange student you know.)

COMPLEXITY: You are a Peruvian agronomist who would like to introduce American agricultural technology to Peru. What new problems might be created as a result of your efforts?

CURIOSITY: You are a chef. Prepare an authentic Peruvian dish. (Copy the recipe and list the ingredients.) How does it taste to you and your classmates? Can they guess what the ingredients are?

IMAGINATION: You are a lyricist. Write a song or a poem about the daily life of a child living on a mountain farm in Peru. Put the words to a familiar tune or compose one of your own (listen to a record of Peruvian music).

chapter 6

EXTENDING THE HORIZONS OF THE GIFTED CHILD

Extending the Horizons of the Gifted Child

It it important to offer enrichment activities to the gifted child beyond those normally available in the classroom. Generally these experiences fall into two main categories:

1. activities that are based on the regular school curriculum but add variety and complexity to studies. These also allow for greater personal expression and development of students' abilities and interests.
2. those learning experiences that use the human and material resources of the community to provide exploratory opportunities not ordinarily available to students.

Individual teachers can avail themselves of parental assistance, utilize special facilities and school staff, and explore community resources as a means of supporting and enriching their classroom program. Efficient and effective use of all these enrichment sources are maximized when cooperative efforts by all concerned parties are involved. Through the combined efforts of a broad-based committee made up of school board members, parents, administrators, and teachers, modification of existing resources can be planned. It is a fact that the needs of gifted students require additional financial and human resources. Extra help from special staff and/or volunteers is a necessary component of such a plan. In view of the economic realities of the times and the limits of a school district's resources, the committee must search for effective means to provide equal opportunities on a cost-effective basis.

A successful plan correlates the regular classroom program with auxiliary enrichment activities. Approaches to providing support services for the classroom teacher in order to meet the needs of gifted children will vary according to a school district's size, needs, and resources. Teachers should be involved in the curriculum development, scheduling, student grouping and identification, and selection of materials for such an enrichment program.

A philosophy of classroom enrichment stresses differentiated curriculum. The gifted students are not isolated from their peers and the core curriculum. They spend a greater part of their day in an integrated environment with provisions made for enrichment. Extra-class experiences extend the core curriculum. Parent volunteers can be of tremendous assistance in developing and maintaining support services of this nature. The enrichment program may be coordinated by a special teacher of the gifted, a regular classroom teacher, the librarian, a reading specialist, or another designated staff member. Interaction with the professional in the classroom promotes a viable program. This may be accomplished through newsletters, conferences, checklists, or other methods of communication. At times it may be practical for the enrichment staff to plan and initiate activities for the gifted children.

The following enrichment program may be adapted or modified by the committee. It deals specifically with enrichment activities that are planned by the classroom teacher. These activities directly extend and supplement classroom learning experiences.

(1) Extending the Core Curriculum

ENRICHMENT CENTER PROCEDURES

Activities in the enrichment center are specifically designed to offer enrichment activities to the gifted child beyond those experiences normally available in the classroom. Opportunities to participate may be offered to individuals, small groups, and inter-age groups. While intended primarily for those students identified as gifted, other students should be included if, in the opinion of the teacher, they may benefit from a particular activity. This ensures an open policy with regard to enrichment activities.

Stress is often placed on cognitive development involving strategies designed to promote growth in creative and productive thinking skills. Teachers plan and assign tasks and materials while coordinating the student's progress and schedule with the enrichment staff.

Materials designed for gifted students should be housed in the enrichment center for the convenience of all. The library is well-suited for this purpose and can often serve a dual function as the center for these enrichment activities. It is suggested that teachers specifically state assigned tasks and materials to be used on the ENRICHMENT ACTIVITIES SCHEDULE.

ENRICHMENT ACTIVITIES SCHEDULE

The classroom teacher often plans special assignments for gifted children, and the librarian, special staff, or parent volunteers are involved in these enrichment activities. This follow-through and assistance may be provided occasionally or on a regularly scheduled basis, such as a special library period once or twice a week.

The following ENRICHMENT ACTIVITIES SCHEDULE helps teachers assign tasks and materials while they coordinate the students' schedule with the person assisting the gifted children. Brief meetings should be held at regular intervals to discuss, plan, and evaluate efforts. These forms may be kept on file for the purposes of monitoring individual progress, planning and reviewing activities, and providing on-going evaluation for the teacher, the enrichment staff, and the administrator. The person working with the gifted children is provided with a section in which to make brief comments on the enrichment session—thereby providing the teacher with valuable feedback on individuals and their progress.

Suggested activities:
completion of tasks assigned in class
in-depth research on a particular topic
pursuit of a child's special interest
simulation games and role playing
skills development activities (research, study, etc.)
small group discussions
mini-courses on selected topics
tutoring sessions
creative writing
use of tapes or special media
newspaper work
book reviews
interviews and polls

writing plays or skits
puppetry
special games

This list is not all inclusive, but it indicates the types of activities that might be pursued by gifted children.

ENRICHMENT ACTIVITIES SCHEDULE

Date:_____   Time: from_____ to_____

To:_____   Place: _____

Student/s

Activities

Special Instructions:_____

_____

_____

_____

Signed_____
(teacher)

Comments/Session Evaluation:_____

_____

_____

_____

_____

Signed_____
(enrichment staff)

STUDENT PROGRESS CHART
ENRICHMENT ACTIVITIES

The following progress chart should be completed by an enrichment staff member for each student who participates in these special sessions. The dates of the reports may be scheduled by the classroom teacher in consultation with enrichment staff.

This chart serves to foster interaction between the enrichment center and the classroom teacher in two ways:

1. It provides the classroom teacher with feedback and vital information on individual students participating in enrichment activities.
2. It provides a basis for evaluating overall progress of the individual student and assists the teacher in planning future enrichment activities.

ENRICHMENT PROGRAM SCHEDULE

Most gifted students spend the greater part of each day in regular classrooms. Their learning experiences are extended to the enrichment center for a selected period of time. The time allotment and scheduling are arranged by classroom teachers in cooperation with enrichment staff.

For your convenience, an Enrichment Center Schedule form follows. It is expected that visits to the enrichment center will vary in frequency, duration, and purpose due to the age and ability ranges of the students.

The enrichment staff will coordinate and distribute a composite schedule after consultation with the classroom teacher.

ENRICHMENT ACTIVITIES - INDIVIDUAL PROGRESS RECORD

Name _____

Grade _____   Teacher _____

Date _____

									Comments (on attitude, peer inter-action, cooperation, work habits)
Showed interest in activities									
Worked independently									
Assumed responsibility in group work									
Set own goals and objectives									
Demonstrated logical thinking									
Contributed to group discussion									
Behaved in a courteous manner									
Organized and efficient in tasks									
Demonstrated creative behavior in use of materials									
Accepted new challenges									
Expressed self in a clear, precise manner									

+ good progress

− improvement needed

ENRICHMENT CENTER SCHEDULE

Times Available	M	T	W	T	F
9:00 – 9:30					
9:30 – 10:00					
10:00 – 10:30					
10:30 – 11:00					
11:00 – 11:30					
11:30 – 12:00					
12:00 – 12:30					
12:30 – 1:00					
1:00 – 1:30					
1:30 – 2:00					
2:00 – 2:30					
2:30 – 3:00					

MC—Mini-Course

* —Discussion Group

  —Grade Level

SP—Special Projects

R—Research

CA—Class Assignment

ENRICHMENT CENTER RESOURCES AND MATERIALS

The enrichment center is designed for maximum flexibility and multi-purpose use. The regular classroom materials are supplemented by additional resources and audio-visual materials for staff and student use. The following will prove to be helpful resources to use in the center:

a portable screen
a 35 mm camera
movies
filmstrips
cassettes
a cassette recorder
records
a phonograph
headphones
filmstrip projectors (regular and individual viewer)
an overhead projector
an Ektograph
a T.V. cable hookup
videotape equipment
games
typewriters (including a primary typewriter)

Additional books, resources, and materials are listed in the Resources section.

EVALUATION OF THE ENRICHMENT CENTER

The enrichment program should be evaluated and monitored as procedures and routines are being developed. Assessment of this nature is a vital element in assuring that support services are benefiting directly both the classroom teachers and their gifted students. The following evaluation forms for teachers and students may prove helpful for this purpose.

TEACHER EVALUATION QUESTIONNAIRE

Review of the Enrichment Center

1. Has the time schedule for the Enrichment Center been generally suitable for your students' needs?

2. Which materials and resources have you found to be most suitable for your students?

3. What additional materials and resources would you choose to add?

4. Has the feedback on student progress in the Center been helpful?

5. What changes, if any, in the schedule and routine would you suggest?

6. What additional activities would you suggest for the enrichment program?

7. Have you noted any changes in pupil behavior, attitudes, or products that can be attributed to enrichment activities?

8. Additional comments:

Student Evaluation Questionnaire

Name _____ **grade** _____

Please check (√) the following activities to tell us how you liked them:

Activities (list)	Very much	A little	Not at all

I would like to spend (check one)
   more time_____, less time _____, the same _____ in the enrichment center.

How has the enrichment center helped you most? (Please check all that apply.)

_____ Regular school work   _____ Learning to use special equipment

_____ Research projects   _____ Extra help & answers to questions

_____ Special Activities   Other ways (please list)

What would you change or add to activities done in the Enrichment Center?

_____

_____

Do you have any other suggestions to improve the Enrichment Center?

_____

_____

Have you had any problems caused by the Enrichment Center? Please describe.

_____

_____

(2) Community Learning Resources

The education of our gifted youngsters is not the exclusive domain of schools and professional educators. Indeed, the community and its citizens must be made aware that schools cannot and should not do the job alone.

The school board, comprised of local citizens, regulates school policy and practices. Such a board does not represent the sum total of a community's involvement, but it does signify the community's responsibility in supporting the education of its future citizens.

Schools do not have a monopoly on learning. They cannot duplicate the vast wealth of human and material resources found in the community. There are extended opportunities for understanding society and developing social and personal values that can best be met by the human and material resources of the community.

Competent and concerned adults can do much to foster giftedness among children of lower socio-economic groups who lack opportunity and exposure to special facilities. Helping to develop positive attitudes and guiding the energy and talent of these youngsters into productive channels is certainly a worthy endeavor.

It is very important for gifted students with disabilities to participate in out-of-class enrichment activities so they will not be handicapped by an inability to relate, work, and function with ease in the community.

Beginning in early childhood, exposure to community learning experiences should be an integral part of the gifted child's educational program. Involvement in community learning will vary in degree and kind according to the developmental needs of the child.

Efforts made by the school and community working together to provide supplementary enrichment opportunities for the gifted will help cement the bond of support for school endeavors. This will also uplift the quality of education for all students.

The following pages cover:
>   an after-school enrichment program
>   a community talent bank directory
>   a school/community mentor program

AFTER-SCHOOL ENRICHMENT PROGRAM

Special-interest classes and workshops provide an excellent opportunity for gifted children to pursue a subject in depth or to survey intriguing new areas. It is not recommended that these after-school enrichment classes be open only to those children identified as gifted. Through exposure to a variety of exciting new learning experiences, untapped talent may sprout and bloom. Self-selection of courses by children encourages a self-identification process of their unique abilities and potential.

How to begin:
1. Form a committee comprised of staff, parents, and interested community members. Select co-chairpersons—preferably one parent member of the committee as the program chairperson and a school liaison person as the planning chairperson.
2. Consider time, organization, and scheduling procedures as a group.
3. Brainstorm a list of possible sources for workshop leaders. (If funds are available, you may wish to hire professional instructors assisted by volunteers.) When you rely exclusively on volunteers, an alternate schedule (e.g., Saturday workshops) may have to be adopted.

4. The program chairperson and committee members contact volunteers, select workshop leaders, and outline course descriptions.

5. The planning chairperson distributes information about the program in school; collects registration forms; and coordinates arrangements for time, space, and materials. Every effort should be made to avoid conflict with other special events. If possible, no fee should be charged.

The course offerings should draw from a kaleidoscope of themes, including:

creative dramatics
an author's workshop
explorations of nature
music
puppetry
science
photography
woodworking
magic
arts and crafts
foreign languages and cultures
computers
math and logic games
current events (discussion groups)

While workshop selections may have to be limited, try to achieve a balanced program (i.e., not all crafts) and encourage children to make a second choice.

PARENT-VOLUNTEER SURVEY FORM
ENRICHMENT PROGRAM

Please share a little of your time, talent and energy to help enrich your child's school program. Check the areas in which you may be interested in providing assistance.
Please return form to your child's teacher.
Thank you,

_____
(Committee for Enrichment Program)

_____ Work with individual child/small group
_____ Media-resource assistant
_____ Library assistant
_____ Helping with special projects
_____ Trips/transportation
_____ Telephone mother/father
_____ Typing, correspondence
_____ Records, clerical tasks
_____ Collecting craft materials
_____ After school enrichment program
_____ Other (please specify interest) _____

_____

_____

- -

Name _____ Telephone: _____
When would it be most convenient for you to help?

_____ Mornings _____ Afternoons _____ Saturday _____ Sunday

How long would you plan to work? _____ 1 hr _____ 1½ hr _____ ½ day
Would you be willing to attend a general orientation session? _____ Yes _____ No
Comments
_____

_____

_____

AFTER SCHOOL ENRICHMENT PROGRAM

Workshop Information--

Starts _____ Through _____   Instructor _____

From _____ To _____

Transporation _____

Materials fee _____ due _____   Instructor _____
(*Indicates materials fee)

Description _____

- -

(Please complete registration form and return to your
child's teacher.)

Registration Form

Child's name _____

Grade _____ Teacher _____

Home Phone _____

1st choice _____   Instructor _____

2nd choice _____   Instructor _____

Signed _____
       (parent)   Instructor _____

Your signature indicates your approval of child's selection
and grants permission to attend workshop. There is no
charge for enrichment program but there is a materials fee   Instructor _____
for some workshops.

COMMUNITY RESOURCES

Communities vary in the nature and type of resources available. Any group wishing to start a school/community enrichment program must:

 review the available resources

 assess student needs

 devise a method to facilitate connection

How to begin:

Form a working committee of staff and community members who are interested in providing extended learning opportunities for bright and able youngsters. Designate a chairperson who will act as a liaison coordinating efforts between community and school.

Develop a list of human and material community resources. Some suggested sources are:

 museums

 libraries

 senior citizen groups

 talented parents or faculty

 state parks and wildlife refuges

 community agencies

 professional groups

 service clubs

 foreign student exchanges

 local colleges and universities

 high school students

 local merchants and industries

 newspapers

 radio and T.V. stations

 special-interest groups

Designate committee members to compile a listing of community services and programs currently available for elementary children.

Publish an ENRICHMENT RESOURCE DIRECTORY, which lists specific details (hours, tours, workshops, contact persons, etc.) that will prove invaluable for teachers and parents alike. (Use the COMMUNITY RESOURCE DIRECTORY form which follows to assemble the information.)

Designate committee members to make personal contact with local individuals who may wish to serve as mentors to individuals or small groups of children within the school.

Follow up personal contacts by sending a letter, a fact sheet, and a personal questionnaire to interested parties.

Arrange an interview for the prospective mentor with designated committee members.

Plan a general information and orientation session for mentors.

Publish a TALENT BANK DIRECTORY listing those individuals interested in working with gifted students.

Plan a staff information meeting with the coordinator in order to inform the staff of program and learning options, such as special-interest workshops, mini-courses, and tutoring.

Designate committee members to work with the staff in identifying gifted students and compiling a list matching these students with human and material resources in the community. (This type of program is generally more suitable for students in grades 4 to 6, but some activities can be adapted for primary grades.)

Plan a general information and orientation session with selected students in order to discuss the options, opportunities, and responsibilities to their involvement in this program.

The two sub-committees working on THE ENRICHMENT RESOURCE DIRECTORY and THE TALENT BANK DIRECTORY will find that many opportunities exist for cooperative efforts in seeking and listing community enrichment resources.

The success of this program depends to a great degree upon the coordinator's ability to organize schedules and maintain an ongoing process of interaction between those most concerned: the mentor, the student, and the teaching staff. It is through the integration of these outside learning experiences that education within the classroom will become significantly more relevant.

In order to accommodate gifted and talented elementary students, the coordinator plans each child's schedule and program in consultation with the classroom teacher. The teacher is considered the key person, and the coordinator must maintain close contact with him/her and provide careful monitoring of each child's progress.

It is anticipated that most of the students' work with the mentors will take place on the school premises. This enables the coordinator and the teaching staff to facilitate and organize learning experiences with a minimum of administrative requirements. This arrangement does, however, place stringent demands on the coordinator to organize space, time, and materials effectively. In addition, an ongoing process of monitoring activities and student progress must be maintained while providing feedback to those most concerned. Enrichment activities involving community volunteers may be integrated into the school day or take the form of an after-school enrichment program.

Mentors may involve students in a wide range of topics, from astronomy to zoology. This will, at times, necessitate student field trips and learning experiences beyond the confines of the school. The coordinator organizes these sessions, secures the necessary permission notes, and makes transportation arrangements.

An enrichment program utilizing community members within the school will vary according to the individual school district's size and circumstances. An alternative to the structured enrichment program described above is also possible. Copies of the directory are simply distributed as resource information to individual teachers to use as the interests of their gifted students indicate a need.

The following sheet may suggest a format for recording and listing available programs. Be sure to include information that will prove helpful to the classroom teacher (e.g., accessibility for the handicapped).

The next section deals with the mentor program and includes examples of:

a letter to a prospective mentor
the Fact Sheet on the School/Community Enrichment Program
the Questionnaire
a page from the TALENT BANK DIRECTORY
the Mentor Schedule Sheet
the Mentor Report

Sections on parent involvement and some suggestions for teachers are also included.

COMMUNITY RESOURCE DIRECTORY

Listings

Place	Location	Type of Program	Recommended Age Group/Size	Hours Schedule	Telephone/Contact Person

Comments (fees,*etc.)

_____

_____

Place	Location	Type of Program	Recommended Age Group	Hours Schedule	Telephone/Contact Person

Comments (fees, etc.)

_____

_____

* Accessibility for Handicapped

SOME FACTS ABOUT
SCHOOL COMMUNITY ENRICHMENT PROGRAM

WHAT IS A SCHOOL COMMUNITY ENRICHMENT PROGRAM?
Individuals in the local community who are involved in supporting and enriching the local school program by sharing their time and talents as mentors provide the foundation of this program.

WHO ARE THE GIFTED AND TALENTED STUDENTS?
The gifted and talented students are found in all segments of society and their abilities, talents, and potential for accomplishment are so outstanding that they require special provisions to meet their educational needs.

WHY IS A PROGRAM LIKE THIS NEEDED?
If gifted and talented students are to achieve their potential, they require expanded educational opportunities beyond the scope of the regular school program. The students need to explore different career options, crafts, ideas, and skills that challenge their abilities. Our children need personal attention, adult commitment, role models they can admire and talk to. The teachers cannot do this without outside assistance. Therefore, members of the community are needed.

WHAT ARE THE PROGRAM'S GOALS AND OBJECTIVES?
The program seeks to provide gifted students opportunities to:
- pursue special interests
- interact with skilled adults who serve as role models
- find productive ways of expressing their talents and versatility
- be exposed to a wide variety of learning experiences
- receive support and guidance in personal growth and development
- develop communication skills
- explore and understand the world of work

WHO CAN BE A MENTOR/VOLUNTEER?
Mentors come from a broad spectrum of society and offer a kaleidoscope of talent. A wide variety of crafts, professions, hobbies, and talents can be drawn upon.

WHAT IS REQUIRED OF A MENTOR/VOLUNTEER?
A commitment to share time and talent guiding students in learning experiences. Above all, a mentor is personally interested in the students and concerned with their individual development.

HOW CAN I BECOME INVOLVED IN THIS PROGRAM?
The following steps are required:
1. Candidates for the mentorship program complete a questionnaire outlining their background and interests.
2. A personal interview is arranged with the local school district.
3. A general orientation session is held for candidates to assess their goals and their ability to relate to a particular age group. Expectations for the program, time conflicts, and scheduling are also discussed.

For further information, contact:

QUESTIONNAIRE:
School/Community Enrichment Program & Directory

School _____

Name_____

Address _____

Educational Background _____

Present Business/Academic Affiliation_____

Other Special Fields of Interest _____

_____

Have you had experience working with youngsters?   Yes_____No_____

If yes, please describe _____

_____

What age group do you prefer to work with?   K-6 Elementary_____   Only Grades K-3_____   Only Grades 4-6_____

PLEASE CHECK THE TYPES OF ACTIVITIES YOU WOULD BE WILLING TO ENGAGE IN AT THE SCHOOL:

_____ Tutor to an individual student

_____ Mentor to an individual or small group of students

_____ Give a short talk

_____ Lead an informal discussion group

_____ Give a demonstration

_____ Show filmstrips, slides, or movies

_____ Help in conducting a field trip

_____ Conduct a mini-course for a small group of students

_____ Other (Please specify)_____

_____

When would it be most convenient for you to help?   mornings_____   afternoons_____   after school_____

How long would you plan to work with the students?   1 hour_____   1½ hours_____   ½ day_____   Other_____

Would you be available for a personal interview?   Yes_____   No_____

Would you be willing to attend a general orientation session?   Yes_____   No_____

Comments: _____

_____

_____

Please send completed form to: _____

_____

TALENT BANK DIRECTORY

MENTORS – LISTING

NAME/ADDRESS	PRESENT BUSINESS/ ACADEMIC AFFILIATION	INTEREST	PREFERRED AGE GROUP	ACTIVITIES	TIME/SCHEDULE
			___ Elementary (K–6) ___ Intermediate (4–6) ___ Primary (K–3)	___ Tutor ___ Mentor ___ Talk ___ Discussion Group ___ Other	___ Mornings ___ Afternoons ___ After School ___ Saturdays ___ 1 hour ___ 1½ hours ___ ½ Day ___ Other

Comments: _____

_____

MENTORS – LISTING

NAME/ADDRESS	PRESENT BUSINESS/ ACADEMIC AFFILIATION	INTEREST	PREFERRED AGE GROUP	ACTIVITIES	TIME/SCHEDULE
			___ Elementary (K–6) ___ Intermediate (4–6) ___ Primary (K–3)	___ Tutor ___ Mentor ___ Talk ___ Discussion Group ___ Other	___ Mornings ___ Afternoons ___ After School ___ Saturdays ___ 1 hour ___ 1½ hours ___ ½ Day ___ Other

Comments: _____

_____

MENTOR SCHEDULE SHEET

To: _____ Date: _____
    (mentor)

From: _____ _____ If unable to keep scheduled
      (coordinator)   appointment, please contact

                                  coordinator at_____.

School: _____   (phone)

        _____

You are scheduled to meet in _____ on _____
                              (place)   (date)

at_____ for_____ hour/s with the following students/group:
   (time)

_____

_____

_____

_____

_____

_____

You have indicated that the format of your visit will include_____

_____

_____

            (signed)_____
                      (coordinator)

- -

Please detach and return to the coordinator.

I plan to visit _____ on _____
                (school)   (date)

at_____
   (time)

I will need the following (please check):

_____slide projector   _____overhead   _____tape player

_____film projector   _____other equipment/materials (please specify)

_____

           (signed)_____
                    (mentor)

Please take a few moments to fill out the report as it will be most helpful for planning purposes.

MENTOR REPORT

Student_____

Activity: _____Demonstration _____Mini Course

_____Crafts Workshop _____Field Trip _____Lecture

_____tutoring _____Other (please specify)_____

Week of	M	T	W	Th	F

Student's attitude _____

participation _____

behavior _____

Additional Comments_____

_____

_____

_____

Date_____ Signed _____
                                                  (mentor)

Parent Involvement

Parents are an important part of any educational program, especially those which seek to provide alternatives to traditional modes of learning.

Encourage parent participation, and you will be surprised at the number of talented and eager mentors you will uncover. Parents can prove to be very helpful in telephoning, gathering materials, and providing transportation to and from sites.

Keep parents informed of their children's schedules and progress and encourage their input and suggestions. A parent awareness and information meeting should be held at the onset of the program.

Dear _____:

     Your child,_____, has been selected to participate in an innovative enrichment program that utilizes mentors or community volunteers. This opportunity for learning will greatly enhance your child's ability to understand and relate to the world beyond the classroom.

     The mentors are selected and screened by the committee and are community members of outstanding talent. They will offer guidance and instruction and serve as role models to the bright and able youngsters selected for this program.

     A copy of your child's Individual Program Plan and a parent permission form are enclosed for your information, comments and approval. We would value any suggestions you may wish to make. Participation in this program is voluntary.

     An information session for parents will be held on_____ at_____. We look forward to meeting you at that time to explain this exciting new program more fully.

Sincerely,

_____
Committee for the Mentor Program

SCHOOL COMMUNITY/MENTOR ENRICHMENT PROGRAM

Parent Permission Form

_____ has my permission to participate in the

Community/Mentor Enrichmen Program at _____ School.

I have reviewed my child's schedule and have indicated my approval by my signature. I understand that my child's performance will be monitored on an ongoing basis by the school staff and that I will be advised periodically of his/her progress and performance. I also understand that some activities will occur away from the school and that transportation to and from the site will necessitate my signing a release form.

I plan to attend the parent information session (____ Yes, ____ No) on

_____ date at _____ School.

Signed,

_____
(Parent)

_____
(Parent)

COMMUNITY/MENTOR TALENT BANK PROGRAM

Individual Program Plan

Name_____ Grade_____ Date of Birth_____

School_____

_____

Selection Criteria   _____

                     _____

                     _____

                     _____

Academic Information   Social Development

Special talent, aptitude_____

_____

_____

Teacher comments_____

_____

_____

_____

_____

Mentor Sessions

Objectives - Goals	Progress-Evaluation

Session Format	Schedule/Activities

Student Conference Summary_____

_____

_____

Signed_____
(coordinator/staff advisor)

Parent comments_____

_____

_____

Signed_____

Mentor Comments_____

_____

_____

Signed_____

Suggestions for Teachers

Working with adults other than parents or teachers provides a new type of learning experience for many gifted elementary students. Youngsters from disadvantaged backgrounds may have experienced little personal contact with professionals and received limited exposure to community resources. It is vital for these gifted children to become involved with community human and material resources at an early age. They must receive adequate preparation in order to feel at ease, enjoy the activities and reap maximum growth, achievement, and other personal benefits.

Consideration must be given to student readiness for placement in this type of program. For the program, the child should already have learned:

Organizational Skills: A student must possess basic competency in the ability to plan, integrate, and organize time, materials, and learning activities without undue frustration.

Communication Skills: These skills must be developed to the extent that a youngster can cope with adult interaction and share involvement in common concerns.

Some of the following suggestions for teachers may promote awareness of specific entry-level skills necessary for successful participation in community learning experiences:

1. Has the child become familiar with various routines? Does s/he possess a working knowledge of specific strategies for planning, working at, and evaluating tasks? In the program, the child will have to deal with:

     schedules
     planning sheets
     work folders
     evaluation procedures.

    Provide ample opportunity to practice and expand these independent learning skills on a day-to-day basis.

2. Does the child possess the social skills and manners necessary for effective personal interaction in a variety of situations? In the program, the child will learn:

     the use of personal titles
     introductions
     courtesy phrases
     procedures for various dialogues
     telephone manners
     how to write follow-up thank-you letters.

    These manners must be dealt with on a day-to-day basis in the classroom as children demonstrate respect and courtesy for each other. A variety of role-playing activities may be used to expand skills and introduce new social situations.

3. How developed are the child's communication skills? Can the child listen with sustained interest, record information, and follow instructions? Can the child deal with adults without undue intimidation? The youngster must be able to convey his/her thoughts, ideas, and opinions. Does the child know how to ask questions and speak up when s/he disagrees with a point? Does the child know how to seek support services and guidance should the need arise?

    Encourage the child to ask questions, discuss things, and express opinions freely in the classroom. Plan to have the youngster participate in regularly scheduled conferences and informal talks with you. Provide guidance and support on a day-to-day basis in the classroom.

4. Responsible behavior communicates positive attitude to mentors and other persons working with the gifted youngsters. Caring for materials, returning borrowed items promptly, and observing routines and guidelines all indicate a true concern for the feelings, rights, and property of others. Classroom experiences must provide a basis for developing positive values and responsible behavior.

In addition to promoting readiness to participate in community learning, the teacher should encourage the child to incorporate these enrichment experiences into classroom learning activities. When the gifted child shares the results of his/her efforts with others, this creates a brighter, happier, more exciting atmosphere for learning.

Maintain contact with the mentor and others in the community learning program. This enables you to monitor the child's social and academic progress. Be flexible about scheduling. Don't create a climate of anxiety or penalize the gifted child by expecting him/her to make up all routine assignments that were conducted while s/he was out of class. This involvement with the community will encourage you to seek extended opportunities for all your students.

School Community/Mentor Enrichment Program

Student Guidelines
You are being given an opportunity to share and learn with adults from the community. This is an exciting privilege and with it comes some responsibilities:
1. Be cooperative and courteous.
2. Please ask questions if you don't understand something.
3. Remember to bring all the materials you need for the activities.
4. Share and help others.
5. Take care of materials and clean up promptly.
6. Return borrowed items in good condition.
7. Plan your schedule and make notes on special assignments.
8. Share what you learn with others in your class.

We hope you enjoy this exciting new way of experiencing and learning. Remember to bring your questions, suggestions, and ideas to the sessions.

Your teacher will discuss your program plan, schedule and activities with you. You will also receive a Student Schedule/Planning Sheet to help you keep track of session activities.

If you have any questions or problems related to the program, please feel free to talk them over with your teacher.

Adapted from the prior work of K. T. Hegeman, *School Community Talent Bank Directory,* (BOCES 1, Suffolk County, NY, 1979)

SCHOOL COMMUNITY/MENTOR ENRICHMENT PROGRAM

STUDENT SCHEDULE/PLANNING SHEET

Student _____

Day	From	To	Place	Session/Activity	Special Instructions/Materials
Mon.	___ ___			
Tues.	___ ___			
Wed.	___ ___			
Thurs.	___ ___			
Fri.	___ ___			

Student Notes/Comments: _____

_____

_____

Selected Resources

IDENTIFICATION

Baldwin, Alexinia. *Baldwin's Identification Matrix 2*. New York: Trillium Press, 1984.

Barbe, W. B. and J. S. Renzulli (Eds.). *Psychology and Education of the Gifted (Second Edition)*. New York: Irvington Publishers, 1975.

Beatty, Walcott, (Ed.). *Improving Educational Asessment and an Inventory of Affective Behavior*. Washington, D.C.: Association for Supervision and Curriculum Development, 1969.

Boston, Bruce O. and Richard O. Fortna. *Testing the Gifted Child: An Interpretation in Lay Language*. Reston, VA.: Council for Exceptional Children, 1976.

Dunn, Rita, and Kenneth Dunn. *Learning Style Inventory (L.S.I.)*. Lawrence, KS: Price Systems.

Elkind, Joel. "The Gifted Child with Learning Disabilities." *Gifted Child Quarterly* (Summer, 1973), p. 96.

Gowan, J. C. and E. P. Torrance. *Educating the Ablest*. Itasca, IL.: F. E. Peacock, 1971

Gifted-Handicapped (Brochure). Chapel Hill, N.C.: Chapel Hill Training Outreach Program.

Gifted Students: Identification Techniques and Program Organization—From ERS Information Aid. Arlington, VA.: Education Research Service, 1975.

Maker, C. J. "Searching for Giftedness and Talent in Children with Handicaps." *The School Psychology Digest*, Vol. V (1976), 508-511.

Martinson, R. A. *The Identification of the Gifted and Talented*. Ventura, CA: Office of the Ventura County Superintendent of Schools, 1974.

Martinson, and Seagoe. *The Abilities of Young Children*. Reston, VA.: Council for Exceptional Children, 1977.

Torrance, E. Paul. *Discovery and Nurturance of Giftedness in the Culturally Different*. Reston, VA.: Council for Exceptional Children, 1977.

Ventour, J. A. C. "Discovering and Motivating the Artistically Gifted Learning Disabled Child. *Teaching Exceptional Children*l. Vol. III (1976).

Wallach, M., and N. Kogan. *Modes of Thinking in Young Children*. New York: Holt, 1965.

AFFECTIVE EDUCATION

Brown, G. I. *Human Teaching for Human Learning*. New York: Viking Press, 1973.

Gowan, John C. and Catherine B. Bruch. *The Academically Talented Student and Guidance*. Boston: Houghton-Mifflin, 1970.

Harmin, Merrill, et al. *Clarifying Values Through Subject Matter*. Minneapolis, MN.: Winston Press, 1973.

Hawley, Robert. *Value Exploration Through Role Playing*. New York: Hart Publishing, 1975.

Hester, Joseph, et al. *Philosophy for Young Thinkers*. New York: Trillium Press, 1983.

Hester, Joseph, Don Killian and Doug Marlette. *Catoons for Thinking: Issues in Ethics and Values*. New York: Trillium Press, 1984.

Howe, Leland W. and Mary Martha Howe. *Personalizing Education: Values Clarification and Beyond*. New York: Hart Publishing, 1975.

Isaacs, Ann Fabe. *How to Teach Ourselves To Be Good to One Another*. Cincinnati, OH: The National Association for Creative Children and Adults, 1974.

Kemnitz, Thomas Milton and Philip Fitch Vincent. *Computer Ethics*. New York: Trillium Press, 1985

The Other Side of the Report Card: A How To Do It Program in Affective Education. Pacific Palisades, CA: Goodyear Publishing, 1973.

Simon, S. B., L. E. Howe, and H. Kirschenbaum. *Values Clarification: A Handbook of Practical Strategies for Teacher and Students*. New York: Hart Publishing, 1972.

Webb, James T., Elizabeth A. Meckstroth, and Stephanie S. Tolan. *Guiding the Gifted Child: A Practical Source for Parents and Teachers*. Columbus, OH: Ohio Psychology Publishing, 1982.

Ziv, A. *Counseling the Intellectually Gifted Child*. Toronto, Ontario: Guidance Centre, 1977.

PROGRAM DEVELOPMENT

Boston, Bruce O. *The Sorcerer's Apprentice: A Case Study in the Role of the Mentor*. Reston, VA: Council for Exceptional Children, 1976.

Cooperman, Bryna, Mildred Fischle, and Ruther Hochstetter. *Teacher Let Me Do It: Learning Centers That Grow*. Buffalo, NY: D.O.K. Publishers, 1976.

DiPego, G. and G. A. Davis. *Imagination Express: Saturday Subway Ride*. Buffalo, NY: D.O.K. Publishers, 1973.

Dunn, Rita and Kenneth Dunn. *Educator's Self-Teaching Guide to Individualizing Instructional Programs*. West Nyack, NY: Parker Publishing, 1975.

Gallagher, James. J. *Teaching the Gifted Child*. (Third Edition.) Boston: Allyn & Bacon, 1985.

Gallagher, James J. et al. *Leadership Unit: The Use of Teacher-Scholar Teams to Develop Units for the Gifted*. New York: Trillium Press, 1982.

Greatslinger, Calvin. *Alternatives To the Ditto*. Buffalo, NY: D.O.K. Publishers, 1977.

Hoyt, K. B. and J. R. Hebeler (Eds.). *Career Education for Gifted and Talented Students*. Salt Lake City, UT: Olympus Publishing, 1974.

Kaplan, Sandra N. *Providing Programs for the Gifted and Talented: A Handbook*. Ventura, CA: Office of the Ventura County Superintendent of Schools, 1975.

Kaplan, Sandra N. et al. *A Young Child Experiences*. Pacific Palisades, CA: Goodyear Publishing, 1975.

Kemnitz, Thomas Milton, Edward G. Martin, Kathryn T. Hegeman, and Joseph G. Hickey. *Management Systems for Gifted and Special Education Programs: A Manual for Cost-Effective Administration*. New York: Trillium Press, 1982.

Keith, B. and S. Hall. *Teacher-Made Games: Any Teacher Can*. Buffalo, NY: D.O.K. Publishers, 1974.

Kohl, H. *Math, Writing & Games in the Open Classroom*. New York: Random House, 1974.

Lawless, Ruth F. *A Guide for Educating a Gifted Child in Your Classroom*. Buffalo, NY: D.O.K. Publishers, 1976.

Lawless, Ruth F. *Programs for Gifted/Talented/Creative Children*. Buffalo, NY: D.O.K. Publishers, 1978.

Lewis, Christine L., Sheila M. Buckley, and Cathy Sarvat. *GEMINI: Gifted Education Manual for Individualizing Networks of Insturction*. New York: Trillium Press, 1980.

Lewis, Christine L., Sheila M. Buckley, and Marjorie A. Cantor. *PEGASUS: Providing Enrichment for the Gifted: Adapting Selected Units of Study*. New York: Trillium Press, 1980.

Maker, C. June. *Providing Programs for the Gifted and Talented: A Handbook*. Reston, VA: Council for Exceptional Children, 1977.

McKay, Ralph H. *Handbook for Principals and Teachers of Elementary Programs for the Gifted*. San Diego, CA: San Diego Schools, 1973.

Renzulli, J.S. *A Guidebook for Evaluating Programs for the Gifted and Talented*. Ventura, CA: Office of the Ventura County Superintendent of Schools, 1975.

Renzulli, J. S. *The Enrichment Triad Model*. Weathersfield, CT: Creative Learning Press, 1977.

Sisk, Dorothy. *Teaching Gifted Children*. Tampa, FL: University of South Florida, 1976.

Torrance, E. P. and R. E. Myers. *Creative Learning and Teaching*. New York: Dodd, Mead and Co., 1973.

Weber, Patricia. *Promote: A Guide to Independent Study*. Buffalo, NY: D.O.K. Publishers, 1977.

Williams, Frank E. *A Total Creativity Program for Individualizing and Humanizing the Learning Process*. Englewood Cliffs, NJ: Educational Technology Publications.

CREATIVITY — CLASSROOM

Askley, Rosalind Minor. *Activities for Motivating & Teaching Bright Children*. West Nyack, NY: Parker Publishing. (Lists numerous special activities and learning situations for meeting the special needs of the bright child.)

Blake, Jim and Barbara Ernst. *The Great Perpetual Learning Machine*. Boston, MA: Little, Brown & Co., 1976. (Supplies answers and directions to where answers can be found for questions dealing with all subjects. Lists other books and materials.)

Bloom, Benjamin S. (Ed.). *Taxonomy of Educational Objectives, Handbook I: Cognitive Domain*. New York: David McKay, 1965.

Bruner, J. S. *Man: A Course of Study*. Washington, D.C.: Curriculum Development Associates.

Cheyney, A. B. *Teaching Reading Skills Through the Newspaper*. Newark, DE: International Reading Association, 1971.

Dawson, M. A. (Ed.). *Developing Comprehension, Including Critical Reading*. Newark, DE: International Reading Association, 1971.

Eberle, Robert. "Problem-Solving Modes of Classroom Instruction." *Educational Leadership*. XXX, 8 (May, 1973).

Feldhusen, J. and D. Treffinger. *Teaching Creative Thinking and Problem Solving*. Dubuque, IA: Kendall-Hunt, Publishing, 1976.

Hegeman, Kathryn T. *Animal Kingdom*. New York: Trillium Press, 1982.
(Teacher's manual and student book for first grade gifted students.)

Hegeman, Kathryn T. *Creative Problem Solving Cards Levels A & B*. New York: Trillium Press, 1982, 1986.
(See also *What To Do?* by the same author.)

Hegeman, Kathryn T. *Our Community*. New York: Trillium Press, 1982.
(Teacher's manual and student book for first grade gifted students.)

Hegeman, Kathryn T. *Social Concept and Affective Development Cards*. New York: Trillium Press, 1982.
(48 Student cards with material for the teacher on the back for primary-age children.)

Hegeman, Kathryn T. *What To Do? Levels A & B*. New York: Trillium Press, 1982.
(Creative problem solving books for young gifted children through grade four; they go with the cards.)

Kemnitz, Thomas Milton, Susan Patterson, and Sharon Zerman. *From Pirates to Astronauts: American History for Gifted Classes, Grades 3 to 7*. (Second Edition) New York: Trillium Press, 1986.

Krathwohl, David R., Benjamin S. Bloom, and Bertram B. Masiq. *Taxonomy of Educational Objectives, Handbook II: Affective Domain*. New York: David McKay, 1964.

Labuda, M. (Ed.). *Creative Reading for Gifted Learners: A Design for Excellence*. Newark, DE: International Reading Association, 1974.

McCandliss, Bill and Albert Watson. *Problemoids: Math Challenge* and *Problemoids: Math Mentor*. New York: Trillium Press, 1983.
(Three sets of teacher and student books provide math enrichment in teaching the strategies of problem solving for grades 4, 5, and 6 for gifted children.)

Meredith, Paul and Leslie Landin. *100 Activities for Gifted Children*. Belmont, CA: Fearon Publishers, 1975.
(Gifted/talented, multi-subject, no grade distinction. Contains assignments that can be used in ordinary classroom situations or special enrichment programs.)

Parnes, Sidney J. *Guide to Creative Action* (Revised Edition). New York: Charles Scribner's Sons, 1977.

Patterson, Jo. *Why Doesn't the Igloo Melt Inside?* Memphis, TN: Memphis City School System, 1973.
(Grades 4, 5, & 6. A handbook for teachers of the gifted and academically talented.)

Plitz, A. and R. Sund. *Creative Teaching of Science in the Elementary School* (Second Edition). Boston, MA: Allyn & Bacon, 1976.

Sanders, Norris. *Classroom Questions—What Kinds?* New York: Harper & Row, 1966.

Spencer, Ruth Albert. *Early Childhood Music Kit: The First Year*. New York: Trillium Press, 1980.

Stanley, Julian C. *The Study and Facilitation of Talent for Mathematics*. Baltimore, MD: Johns Hopkins University Press.
(A study in accelerated math for the gifted.)

Taba, H. and M. Durkin. *Taba Social Studies Curriculum*. Reading, MA: Addison-Wesley, 1979. (Grades 1-8)

Torrance, E. Paul. *Encouraging Creativity in the Classroom*. Dubuque, IA: William C. Brown, 1970.

Williams, Frank E. *Classroom Ideas for Encouraging Thinking and Feeling*. Buffalo, NY: D.O.K. Publishers, 1972.

Witty, P. A. (Ed.). *Reading for the Gifted and the Creative Student*. Newark, DE: International Reading Association, 1971.